Ernest H. Sanders
TWISTS OF FATE
A Hamburg Family 1904 – 1941

Ernest H. Sanders (olim Helmut Salomon)

TWISTS OF FATE
A Hamburg Family 1904 – 1941

Edition**Andreae**

Twists of Fate. A Hamburg Family 1904–1941

ISBN 978-3-869 65-122-4

Edition Andreae, Berlin 2009
© Lexxion Verlagsgesellschaft mbH
Case Number 1-280697821

Typeset by: Christiane Tozman

The German edition of 'Twists of Fate' was published in 2005 as "Heil und Unheil. Eine Hamburger Familie 1904-1941" by Edition Andreae, Lexxion Verlagsgesellschaft.

The front cover illustration shows a reproduction of the painting "Blick durch den Plan vom Rathausmarkt zum Ballindamm, 1938" by the Hamburg painter Julius von Ehren, which appears thanks to the permission of the "Sammlung Hamburger Sparkasse". The file card (excerpt) on the back cover is taken from the "Kultussteuerkartei der Deutsch-Israelitischen Gemeinde in Hamburg", Staatsarchiv Hamburg (522-1 Jüdische Gemeinden, 992 b).
All documents and photographs reproduced in the book are in the author's possession with the exceptions given below. Page 56, upper photograph, shows Paul and Lucie Salomon in the Dolomites (ca. 1936), the picture below shows their grave on the Ohlsdorfer Friedhof in Hamburg. The following documents are taken from files of the Staatsarchiv Hamburg: Page 55: File "Sicherungsverfahren" of the exchange control office of the Oberfinanzpräsident Hamburg against Paul Salomon, 1939-1941 (314-15 Oberfinanzpräsident, R 1939/688); pages 73, 80, 81: Police file on the suicide of Paul Salomon and his wife (Unnatürliche Sterbefälle, 1941/1599).

To Marion, Nina and Peter, who suggested that I write this tale

PREFACE

Several years ago – neither of us remembers when – my son said to me, "Dad, so many things happened to you early in your life, you should write it up." My answer was, "Oh, Peter," and that, I thought, took care of the matter. But ultimately, I found myself unable to disregard so well-meant and responsible a suggestion, especially as I owed it to the thoughtful reflection of an offspring and friend. And so I began this project in 2003.

This tale doesn't go beyond the year 1941 indicated in the title. Originally I had continued it to my time as a soldier in the U.S. Army. But it soon became apparent that there was little justification for extending my story to include the rather insignificant three years as G.I. in the relative isolation of Northwestern Florida. My first 23 years have a quite specific topical cohesion, marked by parents, school, and weighty political developments. They are distinctly separate from subsequent times with their marital happiness and children, as well as professional success. Later events are therefore referred to only to the extent that they were affected by those of earlier years.

I met my publisher in May 2004 at the celebration of the 475th anniversary of my school, the "Johanneum" in Hamburg (Germany). Having read my essay, including various writings of my family, he suggested their translation into German and its publication, which appeared in 2005. My renewed thanks now go to him for also offering to publish the English original. I am greatly indebted to him for his efforts, which far exceed an author's expectations. I also thank Wolfgang Weinzettl for his editorial help with both versions of this book. Elisabeth Remak-Honnef has helped me with her thoughtful revision of my text for which I would like to thank her.

New York, November 2009   Ernest H. Sanders

CHILDHOOD

When a long time ago, on the 29th of June, 1865, my father, Paul Salomon,[1] was born, Brahms was a still quite sanguine young composer of 32; Freud and Mahler were nine- and five-year-old boys and Schoenberg would come into the world nine years later. The last third of the 19th century was, with the exception of the intense and bloody, but relatively short Franco-Prussian war, a time of peace and of rapidly growing comfort, at least for the upper and middle classes. The amenities of life progressed with the rapid spread of technological advances such as railroads, electricity, telephone, flush toilets, and modern sewage – and, on the whole, people were unconcerned about the negative potential of the advances of industrialization.

The first two thirds, roughly, of my father's life (1865–1941) were good and benign times, during which he gradually advanced professionally in Hamburg and married, in 1904 at age 39 – three years older than I was when I married – a young woman fifteen years his junior, named Lucie (pronounced Lootsy) Königswerther[2] (a name that these days has become difficult to deal with when I'm asked for my "mother's maiden name"). We children never found out how they met; "there was this young woman, who slipped on a banana peel, and I helped her up," he said when we asked. They seemed, on the surface, a rather unlikely couple. Vati, though not tall, was very upright. With his mustache, straight nose, blue eyes, unbowed bearing, good sense of humor, and intelligent, authoritative, though kindly way of being, he contrasted with Mutti's bubbly, merry nature and smaller, somewhat plump figure. She would sometimes be vastly amused by something – often something rather inconsequential, so that we would join her merriment in slightly bemused fashion.

Each of them was a highly capable person with almost inhibiting impeccable standards within an inherited strict and rather Victorian moral framework. Their reactions to trends, such as Freud, Schoenberg or Nolde, emerging in the early years of the new century were, not surprisingly, negative and resistant. (That these bewildering new concepts could arise in environments such as Freud's studio, with its thick rug and potted palm, has always struck me as ironically emblematic – as if seen through a prism – of the radical changes beginning to emerge at the turn of the century. The atonally waltz-like beginning of Schoenberg's Piano Concerto [1942] could be said to present a reverse prismatic refraction.)

Nearly two years after their wedding, Hilde[3] (known as Hildi) was born, followed by Lotte[4] (known as Lotti), after a period of seven years. Sixteen months after her birth, Germany and – before long – most of Europe were at war.

The end of that nostalgic age of comfort and late-blooming culture arrived in 1916 with the long battle of Verdun and, two years later, on November 11th, with the Armistice (which we still celebrate, in the United States, as a kind of significant anachronism) and with the abdication of the Kaiser on the 28th. That awful first modern war, presumptuously named "World War", was over. The luxuries of the Edwardian age and of the *Blue Danube* (the waltz – "*leider nicht von [mir],*" as Brahms had written melancholically) dwindled and were succeeded in Germany by an erosive economic instability and rampant inflation, which by 1923 had devalued the Mark by a factor of one billion. (My sister Lotti has a framed banknote from that time on a wall in her apartment, a kind of monetary *Mene tekel upharsin.*) Not until nearly five years after the Armistice was it brought under control.

By that time I was five years old. What a time to be born into and what luck to be young and unaware! On Hildi, however, who was nearly a teenager when the war ended, those years may well have had a marked psychological effect. After the end of the inflation, the German economy improved enough – at least for a fair percentage of the population – that within three years my father was able to move his family to our stately and comfortable town house (and its wonderful garden with fruit trees and central oval lawn surrounded by slim, tall rose bushes and light-brown graveled walkway). But when my mother, two weeks before her 38th birthday, gave birth to me – six days after the Kaiser's abdication – life was somber and burdensome. Later I was informed that my name (Ernst

Helmut) was freighted with nomenclatural significance. *Ernst soll er sein, hell soll er sein, Mut soll er haben* (Earnest he shall be, bright he shall be, courage he shall have). Later still I heard that when I arrived I was told, "We really didn't want you, but now that you're here, it's all right." I don't know whether the fact that I was never offended by that story is due to my phlegmatic disposition; quite a bit of time went by, in fact, before I recognized its implications, my understanding inevitably reinforced by Marion[5] (we married in 1954). It is good to be aware of being a late-born child as the result of enduring conjugal love in dire times.

Before the move to the house, we lived in an upstairs apartment in Sierichstraße 82, where Lotti and I were born. It was a nice building in an upper-middle-class neighborhood. Across the street was a small park with a pond, and at the edge of the park was a fountain, from which Lotti and I were often made to get fresh water in a clay pitcher for dinner. The fountain doesn't exist any more. The hall lights for all the floors of the house could be activated by pressing a timed switch on any floor. The timing, however, was Teutonically rigorous, and if in climbing the stairs you dawdled instead of ascending in a speedy fashion, you would find yourself in the scary dark, groping for the switch after having stumbled to the next level. The apartment house had an elevator, for which, however, I was not given a key. More fascinating for me were the elevators in some of the downtown office buildings known as Paternoster – a string of open wooden cabins, which circulated slowly without stopping. If you missed your floor and didn't want to try to get off on another one, you could ride all the way to the top, where the chain of cabins would creakily shift sideways and descend and perform the same maneuver on the bottom. The name came from the rosary, though I remember that when I asked, I was told it was such a risky system that you'd better say all the Paternosters you could.)

To my surprise and disappointment I have hardly any memory of the apartment, except, to some extent, of the room Lotti and I shared at the front facing the street. The two beds were positioned well away from the window and along the two side walls, mine near the door to the corridor and Lotti's along the opposite wall, with the foot end adjoining the rear wall, in the top corner of which was a fair-sized mullioned window to allow some daylight to filter into the adjacent and otherwise windowless bathroom. There were no showers in those days, but bidets were common, and our bathroom contained one of those mysterious – to me – contraptions. In the evening a curtain was drawn over our side of that window to keep the electric light from shining into our room. Lotti, however, who was quite a bit of a hellion, at times would stand on the rear frame of her bed and, with much barely suppressed merriment, pull a corner of the curtain aside to take a peek or two, when someone was using it. She never, to my frustration, reported the details of her particular theatrical experience to me. I don't think anybody ever looked up at the window from the bathroom – too bad for them – for the sight of those two eyes in that mischievous little face peering down must have been far more precious than anything she could have seen. The only other memory I have from those days is that of my father's habit of coming from the breakfast room with a teaspoon in each hand; one of the spoons had the contents of the cap of his breakfast egg in it, while the other contained mostly yolk. Whoever of us, still in our beds, first heard his footsteps in the corridor, would yell *"Hut"* (cap) and would be rewarded with it; as a rule, Lotti beat me at that game – though now I realize that, with respect to taste and nutrition, the loser was actually better off. My competitive frustration was usually mitigated by a gently resigned phlegmatism. (Much later, when, after the second war, I had for some reason to ask my former *Klassenlehrer* – homeroom – in Hamburg for a letter of reference, he included in his response a remark about *"sein konziliantes Wesen"* [his accommodating nature]).

On the first day of primary school in 1925 I was given the traditional *Zuckertüte* (bag of sweets), a paper cone container filled with treats, which I am sure I liked. After all, family tradition has it that as a young boy of maybe four I climbed a chair to open a wall chest, where I knew my mother kept chocolates, and was overheard in the next room to say to myself, "Now look, there's that good chocolate lying there, and Mutti is going to keep it there until it gets old and grey, and then she's going to say, 'Come here, little boy, I give you something special.' – I'm going to have some now!"

In my first year of school my father and I took the streetcar together to go to the business center, near which was my school. I loved the streetcar and studied its ads (*"Margarine butterfein"* is one I remember – luckily my mother paid no attention to that artificial product), but the glissando noises the electric engine made – upward as it accelerated, downward as the car approached a stop – impressed me enough that I would imitate them on occasion at home. In the beginning, I was surely picked up, but I don't remember this. Later, after we had moved to the house, I often walked home – a considerable distance that took about half an hour – frequently in the company of school fellows, but sometimes alone. Once you had the *Stephansplatz* and the *Dammtor* railroad station behind you, there was much spaciousness and greenery, and the big *Alsterbecken*, the large lake that was formed in the Middle Ages by damming the *Alster*, a little tributary to the *Elbe*, was only an at most five-minute walk away; sometimes it was nice to make that little side-trip. – The *Stephansplatz,* by the way, which is a major intersection, was the locus for Hamburg's first traffic light (c. 1926), mounted in its center on a tall and substantial stone column. We boys were much excited by this new monumental symbol of progress, whose construction we witnessed.

It was in 1926, after the end of my first school year, that we moved to the new address: St. Benediktstraße 27 – not an apartment house; the whole house was all for us! The area had contained a religious establishment in the Middle Ages: in addition to our street name, there were the *Abteistraße* (Abbey Street), the *Nonnenstieg* (Nuns' Walk), and the *Klosterstern* (Cloister Star). There was gaslight for the streets; the wick was inside the glass cupola on top of a metal stanchion, and at dusk every day a man would come, open a little glass door with a pole, somehow turn on or light the fixture inside, and finally close the little door, before repeating the procedure at the next light. Automobiles were of course part of the street scene, but horse-drawn wagons were still common, with the the sound of horseshoes and the less audible by-products of the horses on the pavement. Both sides of the street were lined with large chestnut trees. We developed no social contact with our neighbors. The ones in the attached house on the left were thought to be anti-semites. The neighbor in the detached house on the right (no. 29) seemed nice; my father and he addressed each other as *"Herr Nachbar"* (neighbor) across the garden fence.

Going out through our small front garden, with its magnolia, white and purple lilacs, and hydrangeas, I often went to the sidewalk to spin my top, whipping it into continuing rotation with a string attached to a stick. But more often, sometimes with Lotti, I would be out in the big back garden with its gooseberry bushes on the side, its fruit trees, and our playground in the back, containing bars and a swing. We had a gardener, whom I must have pestered with questions and comments, because one day I thought that he called me a *Naseweiss* (a white-nose, meaning a cheeky little guy), to which I told my family I had replied, *"Und Sie, Sie sind ein Zähnegelb"* (you are Mr. Yellowtooth) – a reply that titillated Lotti and amused and faintly scandalized my parents, when I related the incident. In fact, the actual word is *naseweis,* i.e. nose-wise, the nose evidently having the popular reputation as indicative of verbal mischief – as, for instance, *Pinocchio.*

The garden contained several fruit-trees – a cherry (into which Lotti and I climbed a few times to get some of its fruit, much of which had already been visited by birds), two pear trees, and a plum tree, which to my regret weren't harvested. The plums I tasted had fallen to the ground and were not really worth eating. Outside the right fence and directly adjacent to it was a very tall and sturdy poplar tree that, rustling and swaying mightily on windy days and sometimes turning into a huge burning bush in the light of the setting sun, became for me, seeing it from my bedroom window, a potent romantic symbol, as if waiting to play a central role in a tale that, alas, I didn't have the imagination to invent.

In 1966 my family (Marion, Nina,[6] and Peter[7]) and I stood before the house, and, driven to take another look at that tree, I entered the front garden and the path that led along the right side of the house to a locked and heavy wooden door with spikes on top, hoping somehow to have a reminiscent glimpse of the rear garden. A window opened and a head poked out to ask what I was looking for. Hesitantly and with slight embarrassment I explained, and the tall gate was opened. The garden of course looked quite different and, to my great consternation, the poplar was gone. After our return to New York that year I sorrowfully mentioned to Lotti that the poplar was no more. "What poplar?" she asked. Taken aback, I tried to remind her, only to be told that there never was a poplar. I was dumbfounded and upset. Sometime later – perhaps a year or two – I again mentioned to her that that poplar tree had disappeared. "Oh," she exclaimed, "that poplar tree is gone? What a shame!"

From the garden you would enter the house either by a few stone steps down into the cellar or by ascending another somewhat longer set of stairs to their right – past a lilac bush on each side – to enter one of the prize features of the house, the veranda, from which you could see into the greenery of the gardens in the immediate neighborhood. (The nearest street diverged at an acute angle from the beginning of ours, allowing for enough garden spaces in back of our house, which was in the middle of the block, that in the summer hardly a building could be seen.) When in the spring the outside temperature reached about 55 degrees in the morning, the breakfast table would be set on the veranda, the back wall of which contained the large window of the *Damenzimmer* (salon). Not everybody in the family was as ready as my father and I were to enjoy breakfast in the brisk spring air: whenever it wasn't raining hard, even on mornings when it was drizzling, we might well have our quasi-outdoor breakfast – not necessarily to everyone's equal enjoyment. But it could be a beautiful, truly atmospheric way to begin the day. In the summer, with its very long days, we would generally also have our evening meals on the veranda, where the translucence of the slanting glass roof was usually reinforced by a parallel off-white canvas covering underneath; its length could be controlled with a pulley to shield us from the summer sun. You entered the house through the door in the left wall; it led into the *Herrenzimmer,* which contained my father's desk, two large windowed bookcases, separated by a leather couch, on the opposite wall, and in the far corner his leather easy chair, overtopped by a green-shaded lamp, where he would often settle for an evening's read or, for the short time that I was still young enough, read to me on his lap.

Ordinarily, though, you would enter the house by walking straight through the front garden and up two sets of short steps, through the two front doors. For deliveries and for me coming home from school there was that fork to the right, paralleling the right side of the house and leading to the delivery entrance at the basement level on the left, or, alternatively, forward to the heavy wooden door. When my father came home from work – he was one of the three directors of the main Hamburg office of the Dresdner Bank (one of Germany's major banks) – he would ring three times, and Lotti and I would usually, when we were in the house, dash down the staircase to the main entrance to hug and greet him.

As you entered, the spacious cloakroom, with a washstand and a small separate toilet, was on your right. When there was a dinner party, the maid in her uniform was stationed there to admit the arriving guests and help them with their coats. Continuing forward you would reach the relatively small central hall, lit somewhat dimly by the skylight above the stairwell. The stairs, more or less in the center of the house, began at their far side, leading to a landing, turning to the right along the windowed right wall of the house, and, after a longer passage and another landing, turning right again, led, after some more steps, to the corridor of the second floor, from which you ascended to the third floor, where you faced Hildi's room, with, on the left, a little mansard room for the cook and the maid; it had its own little balcony, with enough room for the two of them to sit and look at the leafy street scene below. (Not that there were all that many opportunities for them to do so; they were worked hard, unreasonably so by today's standards, as my sister Lotti just recently pointed out to me with some measure of outrage.)

Hildi's room was all lilac in color. Next to it, when one walked along the corridor, with the banistered stairwell on the right, was what was known – I don't know why – as the *Waschküche* (laundry room); it had no gas and no stove, its center being taken up with two large skylights – in the ceiling and, fenced, in the floor – filtering daylight to our parents' bathroom below. It contained a deep sink and various laundry and cleaning materials. Next along the wall was Lotti's quite large room, the walls of which were covered by a pretty wallpaper with seemingly random leafy patterns on a white background, producing, with all the light coming in from the garden, a wonderfully bright ambiance. Adjoining hers, with a connecting door, was my room. I entered it through its door at the end of the corridor, facing the maids' room. It was wallpapered in light blue, with a white small-leaf design that, to my frustration, resisted my occasional attempts to discover a pattern. Both of our rooms had white furniture, the only remnant of which is the cabinet – now painted light-green – with its glass-paneled door, that now stands in the "study" of our summer home – an old farm in Vermont. It used to be part of my bedroom furniture. High up on the wall opposite my bed was a framed illustration of the ages of man, based on the famous verse 10 from the 90th Psalm. I have no idea why the decorator (inside or outside the family) put it there; I remember looking at it with detached curiosity. My room was a little smaller than Lotti's, because opposite her door was the door to the bathroom, in which we would take our twice-weekly baths. Leaving my room and passing the bathroom door, you would walk along the banister, which, though apparently wooden, never gave way, even though I would occasionally lean against it to take a look at the depths below. Lotti and I – with Lotti the leader, of course – used to try to jump down the stairs, skipping as many steps as possible and reaching the landing with a big thump. This was a particular challenge on the longer central part of the stairs; not that even she could handle nearly all those steps in one go. I'm amazed that the landings stayed intact under all that abuse.

One feature my parents had chosen to install was what was known as the *Haustelephon*. Almost every room had its own handsome wooden phone box – in fact, an intercom; some of them (not ours, of course) had outside lines. I'm sure it was a sort *of dernier cri* and a useful one, since there was no need for yelled communication, and at first Lotti and I had a great childish time overusing it.

On the floor below was the guest room (below, but of course larger than the maid's room, because that part of the front of the top floor was slightly recessed from the rest of the house); under Hildi's room was the living room, where we had breakfast and lunch, and beyond the parents' bathroom was my mother's bedroom (below Lotti's), with a large semicircular mahogany armoire in a clean Art-Deco style on each side of her bed; my father's bedroom, from the window doors of which he could step out on a large balcony, was under mine. All bedrooms contained washstands. My parents started having separate bedrooms, because my father's snoring, which I could occasionally hear, had begun robbing her of sleep. There was a small toilet under the far end of our bathroom, and next to it, nearer the corridor, was the top end of the dumbwaiter, which the cook in the basement, pulling on a rope, used in order to send up food, for the maid, who had trudged up the stairs, to serve us in the living room.

On the main floor, next to the *Herrenzimmer* and separated from it by sliding doors, was the *Damenzimmer,* soon to contain a lovely new

Hamburg Steinway, on which my sisters practiced for their lessons and the inside of whose keyboard cover presently would be marred by the dried sprayed evidence of their teacher's defective dentures. Lotti's devotion to the piano I seem to remember as limited, but Hildi achieved a proficient level of pianism; I heard her play Chopin's A-flat-major Ballade with respectable competence. After she got married in June of 1932, she and her husband would play duets on their own piano. Next to the salon, at the front half of the house, was the sizeable dining-room, where the formal dinners were served; for those occasions a special cook was hired, to whom the regular cook had to defer (I am sure not unwillingly). The dinners could be quite formal and elaborate; one menu I enviously saw being served from my observation post on the staircase was fillet of beef with sour-cream gravy; for salad there might be hollowed tomatoes stuffed with dressed cucumber. Usually, however, there were leftovers for the next day. After the dinner, the sliding doors between the dining room and the salon were opened for cordials and conversations in the two rear rooms.

The context brings to mind the family custom of celebrating a birthday with a dinner, the menu of which was selected by the celebrant. Usually I asked for boiled beef with noodles and *Eiergräupchen* (toasted egg barley) and lots of parsley for the broth. One year, however, I hesitantly chose to ask for crawfish soup and saddle of venison. When the dinner was served, the family's astonishment yielded to euphoria.

The lift from the basement – to conclude the description of the ground floor – went to a small room in front of the right side of the *Herrenzimmer*, which contained a sink, dishes, and breakfast items, such as dry cereal. (I liked Corn Flakes and Rice Krispies, probably the only dry cereals then available; occasionally I would stuff one of my pants-pockets with Rice Krispies – a novelty at the time – which I would secretly munch during class and share under the desk table with a schoolmate.)

The cellar – really a kind of half-basement, that was reached from the hall by a relatively small staircase – contained the very large kitchen under the dining room, with sufficient window space to give it good daylight (it is now a garage), and the pantry next to it. For quite some time we still had an old-fashioned icebox, whose ice-melt was caught underneath; large blocks of ice were delivered to replenish the supply. There were, further, the coal cellar, the furnace room, and, towards the garden, the laundry and the seamstress's room. Laundry (with the aid of a washboard) and sewing were done every Monday by a seamstress. As to personnel, there was, in addition to the cook and the maid, a day maid, who did not live in.

My little mother, who had energetically put the house together with much vision, taste, and artistry (and money), presided over this establishment with reasonably benign imperiousness, as was on the whole the custom in those days in upper-class society. I can still hear her remonstrating on the phone in no uncertain tone of voice with stores that hadn't lived up to her stringent expectations. It was then a good life – comfortable, safe, sane, and civilized.

There were three ways (apart from walking) to get downtown. In addition to the traditional way by streetcar there was a well-functioning subway-elevated system and ferries: Hamburg, known as the "Venice of the North," is threaded with canals, some of which were serviced by the *Alsterdampfer*, several lines of ferries plied their way through them with convenient stops en route downtown, where, having crossed the big lake of the *Außenalster*, they would emerge from under the *Lombardsbrücke* onto the smaller lake of the *Binnenalster* – always a moment of scenic drama, as you faced the stately downtown buildings and church spires ahead and on each side. The service has by now shrunk to a tourist attraction. At a dock about a five-minute walk from the house we could (not living in a house with direct access to a canal) on a nice day take out our canoe and paddle through some of the canals, past gardens and occasional willow-trees along their banks, or to the *Außenalster*, where every Wednesday evening in the summer there were fireworks. A little ice-cream parlor was on the shore near where I walked home from school.

The Elbe, which provides the harbor for Hamburg, could not be reached by canoe; there were dams and sluices. Once we had obtained a car in 1935, we could drive along its seaward portion, which takes about sixty miles to reach the North Sea. It's where I had my first accident, because my father and I, going for an afternoon spin, had our attention drawn to the river traffic on the left and I banged into the car in front of us. He had planned for us to go on a few days' sight-seeing trip to Westphalia the following week, after determining by telephone that non-Aryan guests would be acceptable to the inns where we were planning to overnight. That was off now, he said, having long been a man conditioned to seeing black. "Nonsense," said my mother, "we get the car fixed and you go." And so it was.

Vati, who was then 70, had tried four times to pass his driving test, but, more than anything else, it was the stick shift that defeated him. Mutti, however, managed to pass it, though she, too, had trouble with the stick shift, as Lotti told me. Once Mutti was driving the two of them downtown, when they were slowed by traffic. "You'd better shift down," said Lotti. "Ach," responded her flustered mother, impotently prophetic, "the car will just have to do this for me." The car stalled, the horns honked behind them, and Lotti, increasingly frantic, got into the driver's seat.

On my mother's side there were only two living relatives. Her unmarried brother, Alex,[8] was an engineer with Siemens in Berlin and visited fairly infrequently. My fondest memory of him is that – I think, on the occasion of my tenth birthday – he sent me one of those new-fangled little piezo-electric desk radios, with which I would often fiddle for long periods of time, twisting the knob, at the end of which the thin wire could be made to touch the crystal in a glass container on the top of the radio, thus producing programs of various radio stations in Germany and elsewhere. Their sister, Elli Fanta (the eldest), was a professional pianist and somewhat eccentric; she was said to take her own little tub along when she went on concert tours. On a visit a year or two after our move, she responded to my insistent begging to play something by giving a reading of Beethoven's sonata, op. 14, no. 2. I was impressed and grateful, but also a little miffed that she offered me what I already knew to be Beethoven's easiest sonata. Aunt Elli had two sons with her husband, whom I don't remember at all and may never have met. One son emigrated to South America, and I know nothing about him; the other, Erich, came to New York with his wife, Trude (who divorced him quite a few years later, going off with another emigrant). Their daughter, Marlene, is a successful writer and since her divorce lives on the East Side of Manhattan; she and I have maintained friendly crosstown contact.

When we were still living in the apartment, my father once took me along to Halle, where he was born and where all but his father and brother still lived. Onkel Oskar, a doctor, had moved to the relatively small town of Gera in Thüringen. His eldest son, Fritz, was a homosexual and so, I believe (without knowing for certain), was his brother Hans, a judge, who had lost his right arm in the war. (He tried for a while to play piano with the toes of his foot or feet.) Hans was a pretty adventurous fellow, whom I still see swinging on and off a moving streetcar with his one arm. Fritz, whom I only dimly remember as having visited once, committed suicide by swimming out into the Baltic Sea and not coming back, as I was told hesitantly by my mother some time later, when I asked what had happened to him.

At the time of our visit with my father's family in Halle his mother[9] was quite old, sitting upright in a black calico dress and with a cane. To my memory, she was rather stiff and not particularly forthcoming – very much a figure from another era; she must have been near 90 years of age. Sharing the apartment, with some financial support from my father, were his three maiden sisters, of whom the eldest – Franziska ("Franze") – was a very smart, sharp-witted woman. She came to visit us sometime after our move to the house; it was December, and, like many of the people we knew, we habitually not only had an elaborate Christmas with a big tree with wax candles and sparklers and decorated only with silver and white, but each of the children also had an *Adventsbäumchen* – a tiny tree no more than c. two feet tall, with four wax candles, an increasing number of which would be lit briefly on each Advent Sunday, until on the last all four sparkled. Tante Franze, having reached the third floor in her guided tour of the house, saw the little fir tree on Lotti's desk and, having been informed what it was and stood for, offered the witheringly witty comment, *"Kinder, seid ihr fromm!"* (Goodness me, you are so religious!)

As young as I was, I understood the mordant quality of that remark. Both of my parents were Jewish, after all – though the type of Jews, so common in Germany since the beginning of the 19th century, that wished and felt themselves to be thoroughly assimilated, non-Jewish and non-religious, if not, in fact, benignly atheistic.[10] I remember the occasionally expressed desire and admonition to purge and eliminate Jewish ways (sometimes described as *"ostjüdisch"*) – not that there were really any identifiable remnants in our family. We were just about like everybody else, upstanding German citizens with political orientation slightly to the right of center. In later years Lotti's husband[11] – Uncle Harry to our children – whose parents were emigrant Romanian Jews, was scandalized by that to him incomprehensible and humiliating abnegation of a major part of one's essence, and it took many intense – "you're full of shit," he would say with friendly conviction – and history-laden conversations to bring him around from incredulity to grudging dubiety. Admittedly, he had a good argument; our family's strictures certainly were, if not anti-semitic, at least judgmentally phobo-semitic.

From my earliest years I recall two notable incidents, as they were related to me later. As a perhaps two-year-old little boy, I'm told, I stopped in front of a building three houses away from ours in the Sierichstraße and, looking at the number plate at its street entrance (88), said *"Ssönes Bild"* (beautiful picture). A year earlier, in my baby-carriage, I evidently sang the pitches of the first phrase or two of *Non più andrai* (the aria ending the first act of Mozart's *Le Nozze di Figaro*), a tune especially loved by my father and which, I'm sure, he whistled often. Music and – later – its compositional shape and structure were to become essential factors in my life. I don't have any memory of contact with music and the piano before our move, but I do from the time the upright was moved to the guest room. Certainly

I must have listened to Hildi playing the piano and while I knew that I wasn't to touch that beautiful new instrument in the salon, nothing prevented me from clambering up on the piano stool in front of the upright. After a short while, I think, I became dissatisfied with my inarticulate experimentation and began trying to read music. At that Hildi came to the rescue and pushed along my feeble, but determined efforts, and before long I knew how. She also taught me some of the rudiments of playing, and pretty soon, as I recall (alas, she is no longer alive to confirm it), I somehow had put up Beethoven's "Waldstein" sonata and tried to play it. The beginning seemed manageable, but then, of course, chaos ensued, and the family decided that I should have lessons, which the teacher sensibly decreed should begin with something rather less demanding.

Inevitably, music temporarily took a bit of a backseat when my parents resolved in 1927 that, particularly in view of my father's age (62), I should try to skip the last grade of primary school and go to the lowest grade of high school (there being no such thing as junior high school in Germany). My father may even already have consulted the principal of the *Johanneum,* the leading Gymnasium in Hamburg, about the possibility of my being admitted the next year to the *Quinta,* if I managed to handle the acceleration successfully. One would think that it might have been easier to start me in grammar school in 1924, rather than as a nearly seven-year-old the next year, but regulations were presumably too rigid for that. The alternative they chose three years later was doable. And so I began my year as a *Sextaner* in the fall of 1928, about three months before my tenth birthday. Hildi, who was then 22, was to supervise my now more strenuous proto-academic life (including Latin); I don't remember how long she played that role – with her customary conscientiousness –, for which she ultimately received a diamond ring from my parents, but certainly it stopped by 1932, when she got married to Franz Friedlaender.[12] (By that time I was an *Untertertianer.* The grades in a Gymnasium, in ascending order, were *Sexta, Quinta, Quarta, Untertertia, Obertertia, Untersecunda, Obersecunda, Unterprima, Oberprima.*) But some time before she gave up her duties, she felt compelled to report a misdeed of mine to my father. I had done some homework, which the teacher returned to me to do over, because, he wrote, it was messy. I complied, and it was returned to me again for the same reason. Hildi decided that this was something she had to show Vati, who, straight, neat, and orderly to a fault, came upstairs and without a word slapped me in the face with the soft-covered exercise book. It was a rare event of drastic discipline; there are only two others that come to mind. Evidently, when Hildi was a young child, my father related something at home that seemed so incredible to her that she spontaneously said, "Vati, you're lying." My father, who had trained himself to become incapable of lying, jumped up, mortally insulted, and spanked the poor kid. The other instance was one of the frequent fights Lotti and Hildi had, when, understandably, his patience finally gave out and he tried to spank Lotti, who was already a teenager. But for each of us, as far as I can remember, there was only one instance.

In the summer of 1929 the whole family went for vacation to a fancy hotel in Noordwijk aan Zee on the Dutch West Coast, mainly to celebrate my parents' silver wedding anniversary on the 11th of July. Hildi had composed a wonderfully spirited and witty little play, in which the three of us were costumed to act the roles of three ladies expecting the arrival of their fourth Bridge partner (Frau Salomon), who was of course conveniently late, as indeed she was known to be at times. The memorized script had us gossip copiously about her and her foibles, with commensurate digs at his. Like everyone, my father had his characteristic share of them, but, his basic pessimism notwithstanding, he also had a witty and spunky side, of which I had an example during our vacation, when we all went on a sunny day's excursion through the countryside in a chauffeured limousine. After a while I started complaining about a headache, and it was decided that the sun and heat were to blame and that I needed sunglasses. The driver was asked to stop at the nearest drugstore, and my father got out and came back with a pair. "How did you do that?" I asked; "you don't know any Dutch." "Oh," he answered, "I just said, 'Een Sunnebrill vor de Jung'" – a quasi-Dutch adaptation (90% correct) of German and *Plattdeutsch,* the dialect in Hamburg's surrounding countryside.

Once in Hamburg, presumably having been told not to eat with my knife, I asked what the reasons were for that inconvenient prohibition. "Well," he said, "there was this case of a man having a meal in the dining-car of a train, and he was eating with his knife; and when the train went around a curve, he slit the corner of his mouth. So he sued the railroad and lost the case, because the judge said, 'If you don't know better than to eat with your knife, it's your own fault if something like that happens to you!'" The logic of that story made sense to me, but I wondered – was he putting me on?

It was in the jubilee year of 1929, four hundred years after the Gymnasium was founded by and named after Johannes Bugenhagen, a friend and associate of Martin Luther's, that I was admitted as *Quintaner. Rector Iohannei,* the principal, was an enormously impressive and admirably enlightened older man, tall with straight white hair, who was the last to follow the old custom as *Rector* to wear a formal morning coat. He retired in 1933. Prior to my admission he had written my father that, since I was entering a class that had been constituted the previous year, perhaps I should, before the beginning of the school year, meet and make friends with one of its members, who lived near us; that was Kurt Laun (later Kurt von Laun), one of the six or seven still living. The two sets of parents later became good friends.

The constant mainstay of the curriculum throughout the nine grades was Latin; inevitably I became fairly proficient, which is more than I can say for ancient Greek, a far more difficult subject that was taken in the last six years. I never became as adept as I would now have wished – little more than the alphabet is left. According to my graduation report and the teachers' comments at the end of 1936, I was a reasonably good student, with an A in Music, two C's, and B's in the remaining subjects, including Math, for which, like my father, I had little aptitude The math teacher, a kind man, sat me down on an afternoon before the final test and, of course without saying so, provided me with the test problem, seeing to it that I knew how to handle it. In sports I was pretty hopeless. I was cowed by the three women in our family who were all excellent tennis players. They tried to start me on lessons – probably too early – and before long I cooked up the excuse that tennis strained my right wrist, interfering with my piano-playing. I was a good hiker, however, and, with my father's encouragement, did some guided mountain-climbing in the Dolomites. One ascent involved scrambling up a vertical wall. I was attached to my guide with a rope – a vital necessity, because once, with the countryside far below, my left foot slipped; he held on for dear life (both of ours), and I regained my footing.

I was fortunate to be a member of a class that even in such a demanding and prestigious school was recognized by the all-male faculty, quite a few of whom were published scholars, as containing an unusual number of outstanding boys. There were no girls. In fact, the whole ambiance did awe me a bit. One day – I may have been 14 – I suddenly realized that here I was living in the land of *Dichter und Denker* (poets and thinkers, i.e. philosophers and such) and, by God, I had never thought anything – nothing significant or noteworthy, anyway. That seemed shameful, and I felt impelled to go out and think. I went for a good walk, sometimes with my hands folded behind my back, à la Schopenhauer, but, realizing after about twenty minutes that I hadn't thought anything remarkable, I went home.

YOUTH

There were a few fairly close friends, but I don't recall not getting along with anyone. Apart from Kurt Laun, there was Rolf Overweg, who, like me, played the piano and lived not too far from us; sometimes he would come home with me, and we would improvise for each other on the Steinway – embarrassing stuff of profound adolescent banality and as shapeless as oysters. But we congratulated each other by saying *"Das war aber tief!"* There was Eckart von Puttkamer (old Prussian nobility), with whom I got together at one of our homes, mostly to engage in strenuous *Raufen,* tough physical scuffling, on the floor or on a couch; he liked it a good bit more than I, but I tolerated it because it was something else and he was a nice fellow. Much later, I think in 1936, after the von Puttkamers had moved to a fancy suburban home, they arranged an evening party for the entire class. I got on the suburban train and watched the increasingly dark and isolated stations go by. Finally, I realized with a rush of dismay, that I had been going the wrong way. I stepped across the next station platform to ride in the opposite direction, and arrived of course quite late and after my parents had received an alarming phone inquiry from my hosts. I was greeted with outstretched arms by the noble lady of the house in her evening dress. My father was, understandably, not amused.

There was Karl-Heinz Pump, a lovely, sensitive boy, who in his adolescence developed a promising talent as a painter and died early in the war, and also Hans Palm, the highly and somewhat quirkily intelligent son of an Italian mother and a German father, who had had a case of infantile paralysis as a youngster and therefore walked with a limp and didn't participate in sports. He and I sometimes walked home together, with me, aware of and a bit awed by his intelligence, as the more passive interlocutor. – After my emigration, he wrote me a postcard suggesting inter alia that I read Tom Wolfe. Much later, c. 1980, our son Peter told me that there had been a phone call from Germany, from a man named Palm. When Peter didn't quite catch the name, the caller said in English, "Palm, like palm tree, monkeys, Africa, you know," which amused Peter. I called him back and we had a lovely brief conversation *("Wie schön, Deine Stimme zu hören,"* he said – how lovely to hear your voice). I hung up with a vague feeling of unease, even thinking of flying over; but I couldn't really manage to do so at that time, for pecuniary as well as professional reasons. Two weeks later I heard that he had died.

The cohesion of the class was a blessing. We all got along well and were happily conscious – though not self-consciously so – of our civilized cameraderie, even though we by no means all came from the same social milieu. Emblematic of the times was an incident that occurred when we were reading the young Goethe's drama *Götz von Berlichingen.* One day our excellent and enlightened teacher of German failed to show up, leaving instructions that we should continue by reading the assigned next portion of the play aloud with divided roles. As it happened, that section contained a famous (or infamous) scatological passage that in most editions was replaced by asterisks and could only be found, in small print, in the appendix. Before we began, an earnest debate, taking up a good bit of time, ensued as to whether that passage should be included. Inevitably, it was anticlimactic when it finally was read.

Far more significant was an event that occurred in the spring of 1934, by which time Hitler and his Nazi regime had been governing for more than a year. Unreflective though I was on the whole, I remember well how, stopping by a newsstand and reading the headlines on the 30th of January in the previous year, I had been struck by the potentially calamitous seriousness of old President Hindenburg's appointment of Hitler as Chancellor. My classmates, however, helped to efface for me the growing menace of the thirties, since I was always regarded fully as a member of this cohesive, intelligent, and highly ethical group. One of the faculty was Herr Meier, who was our teacher of English, and for the last three years also taught French, an elective, for which one had to be in school shortly after 7 a.m. He was far from the most scintillating man on the faculty, but taught us conscientiously, though without the imagination to find a way to accede to our occasional requests to read Shakespeare. He may have been right that it would have frustrated us, for whom contemporary English was still difficult, but at least a sonnet or two would surely have been a welcome and doable challenge. He was, however, one of the relatively few faculty members who already wore the swastika emblem in his lapel. The only other Jewish member of the class at that time was Wolfgang Panofsky, son of the famous art historian, who later was to become one of this country's outstanding physicists. (The family emigrated that year to Princeton, where Erwin Panofsky was to continue his academic career.) Wolfgang – a friend, whom I would visit on occasion – was a lively boy of superior intelligence. It seems that one day that spring he cut up during an English class, annoying Meier enough to send him out to the corridor – already a rather unusual punishment in those days, especially for teenagers. Before long I, too, was sent out, because I had talked with my neighbor. On my way out I heard Meier say, "Always these damned Jews!" In the corridor Wolfgang was nowhere to be seen; maybe he'd gone home. When the bell rang, I went down to the courtyard to have my sandwiches – in solitude, because, to my bewilderment, none of my classmates was there to join me. After some time, two of them came to take me back up with them, unresponsive to my inquiry what was going on. It turned out that the entire class in its collective decency had remonstrated with Meier – I'm sure, politely but firmly – about his remark, which they regarded as quite unseemly, until he agreed to apologize to me. And so he did, as we shook hands, while all the boys were watching.

A year or so later I heard that one of the teachers (with the severely monosyllabic name of Ernst Fritz) – who had taught us Greek and had occasionally, in his quirky way, been quite outspoken in his anti-Nazi remarks to us and to others – was arrested right in school, screaming as they dragged him away. But on the whole, I never felt unwelcome in the school, even though, often under pressure, increasing numbers of my classmates joined the Hitler Youth. In the last year, in fact, one of them became an SS-Man, the elegance of whose black coat elicited ambivalent admiration in some of the students on the few occasions that he attended class in uniform.

Apart from numerous day excursions under a teacher's guidance, among which walks in the *Lüneburger Heide*, large tracts of heather punctuated by isolated conifers, were particularly memorable, we went on two trips. One – in 1934, I think – was a two-week bicycle tour in Franconia and Thuringia (including the wonderful late-Baroque pilgrimage church *Vierzehnheiligen*), organized by that enlightened teacher of German and German literature – a tall younger man, to whom the old Latin saying *Mens sana in corpore sano* was truly applicable. We traveled both ways by train in 4th class (not much better than a cattle car). Our first stop was

Eisenach, with its significant historical associations with Luther and Bach. We stayed overnight in youth hostels. Included in the plan was one night ride, which was my occasion to have a flat; a couple of the guys helped to fix it by flashlight. The only unpleasant memory is that we would at times ride into towns – such as Bamberg with its great *Dom* (cathedral) – that had put up a sign on a building, reading *"Juden unerwünscht"* (Jews not welcome). No one in our group ever commented, at least to my knowledge. In fact, in contrast to the Jewish boy in the parallel class, who, to be sure, had a more assertive and even abrasive intelligence and whom I once saw getting beaten up by some of his classmates, I never experienced anti-semitism from mine. Once, on vacation in the Dolomites with my parents, I went hiking with the son of German fellow vacationers, with whom I got into a conversation about racist ideology. I cautiously expressed some demurs, which he countered with the admiring observation, "Just look at your fine Aryan skull!" I had neither the heart nor the courage to disabuse him. The constellation of fine individuals in our class was an unusual blessing. It was, to be sure, more possible in Hamburg than anywhere else in Germany, because Hamburg was by far the country's most worldly and liberal cosmopolitan city; nonetheless, I was exceptionally fortunate.

The other trip was a truly great experience. One of the teachers at the Johanneum had some sort of connection with a major steamship line in Hamburg and had managed to arrange for our two parallel classes and some of the teachers a low-cost Mediterranean trip from Hamburg on a cruise ship at the end of our year as *Unterprimaner* in the spring of 1936. Each of us had to choose (or was assigned) a topic to research and present before the term ended. I was lucky that mine was Taormina on the Ionian coast of Sicily. The students' quarters on the ship were not much better than glorified steerage, but we had no reason to mind; we slept on cots at night and had a glorious time during the day. Among the many major experiences, apart from Taormina (Goethe's most beautiful spot on earth, to which I introduced Marion in the 90's), was a stop at Malaga, where Palm and I availed ourselves of the opportunity to take a memorable side-trip to Granada. But there was a palpably ominous atmosphere pervading our Spanish interlude. The country wasn't far from its civil war, and our ship with its swastika flag was received with surly unfriendliness.

After visits to Spanish Morocco and Tunis and a side trip to Gabès at the edge of the Sahara, with sabered Bedouins giving whirling equestrian demonstrations, we stopped in Malta, Sicily, and Naples (where one of the guys arranged for some of us to watch a private show in a whorehouse that left me depressed), before returning by train from the French Riviera.

Several years earlier, in 1931 or 1932, I had caught nephritis, a not uncommon illness for pre-adolescents, that is serious enough to require several weeks of bed rest. One of its symptoms is an excess of albumin in the urine; as a result of the customary sloppy reference to "albumen," people, professionals and non-professionals, would refer to it as *Eiweiß* (egg-white). I was confined to bed for the better part of six weeks; toward the end of that time I noticed a quite pleasant discharge of whitish fluid. "That's quite a bit of *Eiweiß*" I thought, "I must be getting better," especially since this kept happening off and on. It didn't take me long to realize that, while I probably was recuperating, what was happening was no overproduction of albumen. My father came up after a few days, undoubtedly having been told by my mother about the evidence of this new development. I remember him sitting by the window, looking out into the neighborhood and saying something about what he had heard, but his abashed Victorian sense of propriety prevented him from making any sensible contact. Like many others, I ultimately got my enlightenment from reference books, in my case from the multi-volume encyclopedia he had in the *Herrenzimmer*.

Karl-Heinz Pump and I once, several years later, found ourselves in a restaurant or bar, where he, with his painter's eye, observed a young woman in a white blouse and a green cardigan, buttoned low, so that it accented the front of the blouse – not provocatively. "That's how they do it," said Pump – or words to that effect. "But she's not really showing anything," I objected. "Never mind," he said, "she's calling attention to herself as a woman." I was still naive enough to be somewhat mystified, but felt myself instructed. By then the Nazi time was in full swing. "Aren't there any Jewish girls that you could get together with?" he asked in a voice of kindly concern.

It was a problem. I was shy and awkward with girls; moreover, to the extent that our family's acquaintances had any daughters, they were of course older, and my parents' strictures about Jewishness, as well as the absence of any girls in school interfered with that part of my adolescent development, which didn't really begin until I was in my nineteenth year. The widow of one of my classmates told me recently how they had met on our class cruise. One of the teachers had noticed that a group of girl passengers had congregated on a deck below the one where some of the boys were idly spending their time. He told them that he couldn't see why they didn't take advantage of the opportunity for female company. And so some of the guys went down, including August-Wilhelm Hewicker (called "Auwi" by us), who went straight to her. There never was anybody else for either of them, and in due time they got married. The racial policies then prevailing in Germany prevented me from pursuing that sort of approach – no matter what the ultimate outcome might have been.

There was, however, music. Before my voice changed, I had a lovely boy-soprano, which at times I would get going at the stairwell on the top floor of our house, creating improvised coloratura jubilations. My love-affair with music, however, had begun earlier with my infantile pianistic struggles. We also had a wind-up phonograph with a rather haphazard record collection. I was particularly entranced by the Minuet of Mozart's String Quartet in d-minor, K. 421 [417b], the second of the "Haydn" quartets. I must have heard some orchestral music at a fairly early age, because I recall occasionally standing at a sunny spot in the garden, where I could watch my shadow and, conducting an imaginary orchestra with a wooden garden stick and humming, with appropriate emphases, music I knew or improvised, provided affectionate amusement for whatever family members might see me. In Westerland auf Sylt, a seaside resort on a North-Sea island off the coast of Germany just south of the Danish border, where Mutti and her children (at least the two youngest) used to spend several weeks in most summers, the local *Kappelle* (small orchestra) gave afternoon concerts in a raised band shell, below and in front of which this little boy would often position himself and co-conduct, oblivious to the amusement and perhaps annoyance he must have given to the public and to the conductor.

My piano lessons continued for a couple of years or so, until our teacher died, causing me grief that I tried to sublimate into primitively improvised, but heartfelt instrumental *Traueroden* at the piano. My parents then must have made inquiries, because in due course I resumed weekly lessons, with Wilhelm Ammermann, who was reported to be the best piano teacher in Hamburg and was, in fact, an excellent musician. He recognized and supported my talent, which through inclination as well as my only moderately disciplined approach to the keyboard was always more musical than pianistic. When, after many years' interruption, I had resumed my piano studies after the war, my teacher at the Juilliard School was impressed by pencil markings Ammermann had left in some of my piano music.

I owe Ammermann a great deal. He introduced me to a wide range of literature, including Bach's *Inventions, The Well-Tempered Clavier,* the "Italian Concerto," the d-minor keyboard concerto; Mozart's piano music, including the A-major and d-minor Concertos, and that wondrous a-minor Rondo of his late maturity; some of Beethoven's sonatas; Brahms's two Rhapsodies, op. 79, which – especially the one in g-minor – I handled quite well; later he even put me to work on his Handel-Variations; and some of Chopin's *Mazurkas* and *Nocturnes*. He also taught me at least the rudiments of theory – i.e. harmony – and once gave me an assignment to transcribe the – admittedly "quartetish" – slow movement of Beethoven's piano sonata, op. 2, no. 2, for string quartet. I loved this "extracurricular" job, and he was pleased with my product.

At times, however, he had reason to be less pleased with my weekly progress at the keyboard, which in part may have been due to what seemed to me an inherent clumsiness of my left hand and in part to my at least occasionally insufficient preparation. He'd be upset, but in many such instances he'd then pull out a volume of four-hand duets, and we'd read through original four-hand music or through transcriptions of orchestral music, with me always playing *secondo*. Once – it was already the mid-thirties – he closed all the windows and curtains and put a four-hand arrangement of Mahler's Fourth Symphony on the piano desk, a composition that of course could no longer be played by German orchestras. I owe to him the very exciting and somewhat risky revelation of a composer whose – then relatively contemporary – work (and particularly that symphony) has always impressed me a great deal. By then I had become a very good sight-reader, largely because I was spending a good bit of time at home reading through repertoire (both for two hands and the *secondo* parts of music for four hands – with occasional glances and grabs at the *primo* parts). I spent many wonderful hours at the baby grand in the *Damenzimmer,* after first carefully closing the sliding doors between it and the *Herrenzimmer.* And I hardly ever got any interferences or interruptions. That is how, for instance, I became intimately acquainted with the *Well-Tempered Clavier.*

From a relatively early age I attended orchestral and chamber-music concerts. The first performance I heard of Beethoven's Ninth Symphony, conducted by Karl Muck, of course impressed me enormously, and I began to buy miniature Eulenburg scores and study them, while trying to read transposing instruments with the help of mentally superimposed C-clefs. My interest in musical structure was stimulated at Juilliard and Columbia, particularly when I had the great good luck to inherit the undergraduate symphony course, while still a graduate student in the 1950's. One winter afternoon I happened to be listening to a performance of Beethoven's String Quartet op. 127 on the radio in the living room. I hadn't heard it before and, as the daylight gradually dimmed, I experienced the slow movement with a memorably overwhelming intensity. Similarly, I remember the miraculous shock my first live exposure to Schubert's String Quintet gave me. I was transfixed, and since customarily one could buy miniature scores of programmed works in the lobby before or after a concert, I bought one right after the performance to study and own it. I still have it as well as many others I acquired during those years. When returning home after such stirring occasions I would at times try more or less successfully to avoid conversation by sneaking up the stairs, being persuaded in my self-conscious adolescent intensity, verging on arrogance, that I couldn't possibly let the familiar contaminate the extraordinary.

Another noteworthy experience was the concert Otto Klemperer conducted on the 30th of January, 1933 – the day the Nazis began their rule of Germany. I hadn't heard him conduct before, because he had avoided Hamburg for sixteen years after a scandal, late in 1912, involving a married woman and her cuckolded husband, who had shouted at him from the front row of the opera to turn around and, as Klemperer did, horsewhipped him in the face. It was an all-Beethoven concert, with Edwin Fischer's wonderful performance of the Third Piano Concerto framed by the Second and Fifth Symphonies. The Fifth even then was of course well over a century old, but it was still fresh, certainly for me and especially under Klemperer, who was then rather a wild man and, being tall, conducted without a podium and without a score, allowing him to take an occasional step or two into the orchestra and demonizing the musicians into superb performances. Two months later he had emigrated. Marion and I heard him in his old age, sedentary and slower in gait and tempo, but still compelling, a couple of times in London in the 60's and once in New York.

My response to opera was less successful, even though opera was a high-class entertainment for our family, especially for Hildi, who was an enthusiastic and quite literate opera-goer. "Well," they thought, when I was about eight years old, "it's time the boy gets introduced to opera." But easy does it – nothing too demanding to begin with; and so it was decided that they should take me to Auber's *Fra Diavolo,* presumably having prepared me with a summary of the story, to which I suspect I didn't pay excessive attention. I sat through the performance, of course, but, my, what a bore! It took a long time (close to three decades) to wean me from my disregard of opera, and I have always regretted the relative superficiality of my knowledge of Wagner's masterworks. But then again, to a greater or lesser degree, I share less than thorough knowledge of and insight into Wagner with quite a few more or less sophisticated music-lovers.

All too soon the few happy years of the later twenties began to yield to increasingly worrisome events. The American Depression, the first major economic disaster since the end of the German inflation six years before, was not followed by comparable symptoms in Germany until two years later. They were serious enough, however, that my father called my mother and me home from our summer vacation in the Harz mountains. He was late coming home from the office on the day of our return, and I was already in bed when he came up to give me a good-night kiss on the cheek – a rather unusual gesture by that time of my life. A measure of the seriousness of the situation that I recall was the scratch of his facial hair; for once he evidently didn't get his shave that morning, probably having worked through the previous night.

In the summer of 1932, not too long after that scare had passed, the Johanneum's music teacher, with the Silesian, near-Slavic name of Tzschaschel, and his wife took some of the boys in my class, including me, by hired open-air truck on a four-week vacation in Scharbeutz, a Baltic seaside resort, where we had a great, carefree time. On one of those days I was idly lying in the sand and talking to him. I groused about my surname; I didn't like it, I told him. He tried to dissuade me: "It's such a beautiful old Biblical name," he said with, I'm sure, the best intentions. But I knew better and clammed up. Once, on an excursion, I had been teased by our *Klassenlehrer* for the lower grades. *"O Salomon, o Salomon, was bist du doch für'n kleiner Cohn"* (you are indeed a little Cohn).

It was in the futile attempt of preparing against impending anti-semitic policies in Germany that my father one evening later that year interrupted me at the piano to tell me that, largely for the sake of any protection it might give me, he and Mutti had thought that it might be a good idea if I were to replace the non-religious tradition of our family with the Lutheran Protestantism of Northern Germany. What did I think of getting baptized? I was 13 and wasn't really thinking anything, except that perhaps it would help me to narrow the distance in that area between me and my classmates. In any event, I'd been participating in religious instruction and in singing the many beautiful traditional hymns with them. So, that proposal seemed just fine to me, and I was put in the charge of Pastor Hunzinger, an intense, fairly young man, who was reputed to be a political liberal. He had me over to his rectory downtown, where, in the dimness of the declining daylight of the season and with the fire glowing in the tiled oven, he would instruct me, his eyes intently fixed on me. He may have been and probably was a political liberal, but in religion he was a strict Lutheran. Those were magically impressive afternoons, and he did his job well; I was instructed and fully converted. A couple of years after my baptism, which my parents must have attended with quite mixed feelings, I was confirmed. I went to church, where he delivered highly intense sermons, and one day I said to my father, "You know, he's really quite terrific; come along with me next Sunday." That, of course, was a development he hadn't envisioned, but he did go with me and sat apart from me in the back of the nave, hat in hand. I then realized the futile and poignant absurdity of the situation and never asked him again.

Later, in New York, I went to a few Lutheran churches, but it wasn't the same sternly uplifting experience. Only once, when as a G.I. I attended a properly traditional service in a village church in Germany, I experienced similar stirrings. But I was adrift. In the summer of 1945, walking in Wiesbaden, I passed a church, whose pastor was identified on the door as Walter Hunzinger. I of course hastened to follow up this miraculous coincidence, found his apartment, and went to visit him (and his wife and five children) in my uniform. Great astonishment and smiles, and much conversation, in the course of which he asked the oft-heard question, "Was it really necessary to destroy our beautiful cities so terribly?" Not being able to answer, I deflected the question by with naive optimism pointing to the fundamental changes to be expected with the recent institution of the United Nations. *"Friede auf Erden?"* he said, *"daran glaub' ich nicht."* (Peace on earth? I don't believe it.) The new millennium daunts contradiction.

One day, perhaps about 1935, I came home from a piano lesson and, glowing with excitement, told my mother, "Do you know what Herr Ammermann said to me today? He told me that I'm his most talented student!" "Ach," she said, "he just wants to have his bills paid." I may have realized even then that she was scared about my possible future as a musician, especially in those increasingly threatening times. In any event, early in 1937, I think, came the time that he sat me down at a small table and, after having poured cognac into two glasses, regretfully told me that, circumstances being what they had become, he just couldn't risk continuing to teach me. I had always had a thick skin, which perforce had become even thicker in the course of the thirties, and I responded that, for sure, I was sad, too, but that of course I understood; in any case, I said, I knew that not too long hence I'd have to leave Hamburg. Less than ten years later I was told that he had died during the massive fire-bombing of the city in 1944: covered with flames, he drowned after jumping into a canal.

Under the pressure of the "Thousand-year Reich" to speed young men into the armed or other uniformed services, our class was the first whose graduation had been advanced from Easter to the preceding Christmas (1936). Non-Aryans, of course, were privileged to be deprived of serving the increasingly aggressive fatherland. That I had been in danger of forfeiting my *Abitur* (graduation) was an eventuality of which I remained unaware for 46 years. Early in 1981 *Das Johanneum,* a small quarterly of about 20 pages, published a historical essay regarding trends and events in my school during Nazi times. Not surprisingly, the author knew nothing

Helmut Salomon's certificate of baptism and confirmation (November 16th, 1932 and March 25th, 1934)

about my and my classmates' encounter with Meier. Of course I felt that I should report it as an addendum, but in the course of the demands of life with a wonderful family and preoccupied with academic duties (publications, as well as chairmanship and teaching in the Department of Music at Columbia University) I procrastinated long enough to come across the following contribution nearly two years later. After relating the class's remarkable intercession with Meier, the writer (Joachim Brandis), having cleared his report with the other classmates surviving in Germany, narrates circumstances and events in the autumn of 1936:[13]

> […] At that time, it seems, an order had been issued interdicting graduation for Non-Aryans, in accordance with the Nuremberg laws. […] Consequently the class's principal teacher informed the students [evidently in my absence] that Salomon presumably could not be allowed to graduate. […] This information at first caused disquieting incredulity, followed by indignation. The class, in accordance with its tradition of confronting critical circumstances with ironclad unity, discussed what could be done to avert the threatened fate from its classmate, with the result that the speaker of the class was charged to go, in his Hitler-Youth uniform, to the school's director with the straightforward declaration of the class request that Salomon not be excluded, but take the final examination jointly with everyone else, for the reason that throughout the years from *Quinta* to *Oberprima* he had proved to be an impeccable classmate and that the class as an entity would be dismayed by the sudden exclusion of one of its members. [At a gathering of the remaining members of the group in 2002 I asked Kurt Laun about the background of this action. He told me that they had a meeting to discuss the case; the course of action was determined and submitted to a vote, which was unanimous, except for one abstention.] The speaker of the class having executed his mission, Salomon without further ado took the exams jointly with the class. [Credit is of course also due the director of the school, who, evidently having some latitude of action and surely concerned about undue publicity, gave in to the pressure. Like all my classmates, then, though unaware of their virtuous deed, I walked up the steps to the podium in the great hall when my name was called – "Helmut Salomon" – shook his hand, and received my diploma.] The German *Abitur* enabled him to study music in the USA. […] *(my translation)*

The preceding sentence fails to convey the full extent of my debt to my classmates. A G.I. since October, 1941, I was sent to the Frankfurt area of Germany by the Army, leaving New York on V-E Day, after having, at the Army's suggestion, changed my name, because before the end of the war my citizenship, granted in April, 1943, was thought quite possibly to be insufficient protection.[14] I began to realize sometime after the beginning of my hedonistic life there that I should come to a decision about my post-military career. For its first 15 months after my discharge on 21 February,

Diploma of having passed the German Abitur at the Johanneum (February 1st, 1937)

1946, I continued to live in the Frankfurt region as a civilian employee of the Army, induced by love, a carefree life, and good pay for little work. Mrs. Eberstadt (the wife of one of my father's former colleagues, who in 1936 had emigrated with his family to London) had urged me in early January of 1946 to look up her sister-in-law in Frankfurt, who, as the recently widowed wife of a non-Jewish husband, had come through the war O.K. She took me across the street to meet the family of her son's fiancee, who as well as her father and her sister were all musical and amateur instrumentalists – flute, piano, and violin. They welcomed me instantly, we played chamber-music and four-hand piano duets almost every weekend, and before long the younger daughter, lovely and spirited and not yet 17, and I fell in love. As time went on, the lure of music as a profession became irresistible, and for a year or so before my return to New York in May of 1947 I took piano lessons in Frankfurt.

Having applied to the Juilliard School of Music for admission in the fall, I enrolled in its summer school for six weeks of lessons. Even though I was a nervous wreck before, during, and after my entrance exam in September, the jury evidently heard something they must have thought worth cultivating, for – as I heard later – they called in my teacher to ask if he thought that he could "fix me up." He said that he thought so, but less than three years later he kindly, but definitively recommended that I go to Columbia University for graduate work in historical musicology. There I was given the devastating news by someone in the Department of Music that, having attended a conservatory, I lacked two years' worth of undergraduate academic credits. I had in the meantime used up three fourths of my financial entitlements for educational expenses under the "G.I. Bill of Rights" and had no idea how I was going to cope. A few days later I got a phone message to see the Dean of Graduate Studies at Columbia, who informed me that I was entirely acceptable to them as a beginning graduate student. When in my overwhelmed bewilderment I asked, in effect, "How come?" he said the major factor was my having an *Abitur* from an outstanding Gymnasium. It was my great good luck that the dean was also a German refugee; forwarding my dossier to the formerly European head of musicology, he wrote on it *"Grabben Sie ihn"* in droll fractured German (grab him), as the latter later told me. Actually, I was lucky in more ways than one. The review of my one public appearance – in Brooklyn in 1949 – had mentioned me as "the generally reliable accompanist." Historical musicology equipped me and my musicality to bring to bear a committed concern on aspects of a great art, arising c. 1200, that no other civilization has equalled in complexity and intrinsic significance.

Before the account of my "political" experiences at my school during the Nazi years was published, one of my former classmates – presumably the author – was delegated by them to send me a copy for my approval, which I was much moved to give. The first sentence is translated here from the original German:[15]

> The far-reaching consequences of such an experience, with its exemplary humanity (in the best sense of the word – with great honor ultimately due also the *Gelehrtenschule des Johanneums*) and in a historical situation in which your action bestows a very special definition on the word *"Zivilcourage"*, have given my life significant determination [...] It's a good story – in the best sense of that expression. I've never ceased to realize how lucky I was.
> <div align="right">Ernest H. Sanders (olim <i>Helmut Salomon</i>)</div>

I should have added that my fellow students greatly contributed to my disposition to try, in evaluating an individual, to avoid any prejudicial contamination, i.e. to do so, in the words of Tacitus, *sine ira et studio*.

I feel compelled to add a postscript to this tale of unselfconscious decency, liberalism, and courage in the face of immensely challenging circumstances. In the spring of 1937 I was asked by a few of my ex-classmates, who were still civilians, whether I might like to join them in a trip to Yugoslavia. I consulted with my parents, who may have had their compunctions, but didn't categorically advise against it. Not much later, however, I heard Hans Palm with his slight limp come up the stairs to our living room to convey to me with sorrowful regret their conclusion that it wouldn't be good or safe to have me join them. I'm not sure that in the end any of them took the trip. (In the summer of 1970, in a compulsive act of historical adjustment, while my family and I were spending a second academic year in England for my musicological research, I took the four of us on a vacation trip to Southern Italy and Yugoslavia. Deservedly, during a rough nocturnal crossing of the Adriatic from Bari to Bar, I heard our eleven-year-old daughter complain about "stupid people, who want me to go traveling!")

The first time I saw some of my classmates again after the war was in August 1945, when as a G.I. I hitch-hiked from Frankfurt to Kassel, where, some service just having been resumed, I caught a rather dilapidated and unlit overnight train to Hannover in the English occupation zone. I hailed a British lorry, whose driver agreed to let me ride with him to Hamburg, and looked up the Launs, still in our former neighborhood, which hadn't been smashed too badly. They corralled those who had survived and returned. It was a heady experience for all of us.

In the last few decades I have attended some of the annual summer meetings of our diminishing group. The few remaining octogenarians are all friends; one – Kurt Andreae, during his service as German consul in Philadelphia – initiated an enduring close friendship between our two families in the 1960s.

After graduation and almost simultaneously with the end of my piano lessons I became an apprentice in a private – still Jewish-owned – Hamburg bank firm. My father, who had been retired in 1933 on his 68th birthday, thought that, particularly in view of the political developments, I should have some practical training and grow a bit older before any more decisive career move. In less troubled times he had thought of me as going into the legal profession, perhaps becoming a judge – with music. I spent a year and a half at the bank, with limited interest and limited acquisition of useful knowledge. Conditions had been deteriorating ominously in Germany. My sister Lotti knocked herself out to convince our parents that it was late, but not too late, to leave, but they – especially my father, who was then 72, though my mother was only 57 – understandably didn't have the flexibility (they would, perhaps rightly, have thought of it as foolhardiness) to be persuaded by her arguments. Theirs were primarily that they were too old and that they would be a burden on their children, especially my father who had never been good with his hands; he couldn't wrap a package, and after a few attempts in earlier years to shave himself – which were a bit of Grand-Guignol theater for us ("Look at the blood!") – had always reverted to having a barber come every morning from the barbershop a ten-minute walk from us. Moreover, the murderous percentage the Nazis charged for export of money would reduce his assets to ten percent. Lotti has always insisted that we would have managed somehow.

But they stayed, and we left. Lotti went to New York in March 1938; Hildi, her husband, and their four-year-old daughter Inge went to England a month later, to the God-forsaken town of Bradford in Yorkshire, which was a prime locus for his business (the wool trade); and I, having been moved to the living room after their departure, followed Lotti in October, leaving my desolated and relieved parents standing on the railroad-station platform, waving their good-byes.

EMIGRATION

Before leaving home I still had a special noon-time dinner with my parents, expertly prepared by my mother, who knew that *Seezunge,* an especially delicious kind of North-Sea sole, was one of my favorite dishes – the more so as, being expensive, it wasn't served very often. The fillets were always cut into fairly small slices, which were rolled into bite-sized pieces, each stuffed with a small North-Sea shrimp and served with a white sauce. I have a rather precise memory of the occasion, with the three of us sitting in our accustomed places at the dining table and the room lit dully by the light of a cloudy fall day.

Unlike my sisters, I left by train, because I was going to spend two weeks with Hildi and her family in Yorkshire. Shortly before the day of my departure from Hamburg it had been decided that for the trip to Hoek van Holland (for the overnight ferry to Harwich) I should take the later of two trains, which was rumored to be subject to less stringent and perhaps traumatic examination of Jewish emigrants. The parting from my parents left me, who had always had a (North-German?) tendency toward emotional reticence, in a state of bewildered psychological numbness.

By that time – it was October 14th, 1938 – there were relatively few people riding into Holland, and as the train approached the border, I was the only passenger in the six-person compartment. A while after the train had stopped, two SS-men entered, closed the door, and drew the curtains. They examined my wallet and my documents, including my passport, which had been stamped its front page with a red J, had me remove one of my shoes (it was known that some emigrants had tried to smuggle out valuables in the shoes they were wearing) – and left. It was an anxious few minutes, but after a while, to my great relief, the train started to move across the border. I reopened the curtains.

I had eleven fall days with Hildi, Franz, and little Inge, who, not yet five and recently having had to experience separation from her home and her grandparents – Vati was her loving and beloved "Apapa" – was happy and excited to see a member of her disjointed family. An odd lack of mnemonic precision beclouds that interlude for me. It isn't, I think, that I was insensitive and callous, but that the thick skin I had protectively developed dulled the emotional intensity and memory of the experiences of my final European fortnight. I'm sure that my departure by train on the 27th must have been a lacerating experience for all of us – especially for Inge, for whom, in tears, the recent trauma of disorientation and loss was reinstated and reinforced.

I spent that night in London with the Eberstadts. George Eberstadt, 22 years younger than my father, had been one of the three directors of the Dresdner Bank in Hamburg, and his son, Walter, also a *Johanniter,* and I had occasionally got together in Hamburg, though I had had no contact with him in school, since he was more than two years younger. I didn't meet up with him in London since he was off at boarding school. The one thing that sticks in my mind from my stay in London was Mrs. Eberstadt's "Breakfast!" call the next morning. It was decidedly English, and I realized that I was getting a one-word hortatory foretaste of the routine use of what was to become my second – and before long my first – language. I had had a number of private English lessons in Hamburg, which didn't turn out to be very helpful; it is undeniable that only daily immersion in the active use of a foreign language makes one fluently conversant. I took the train to Southampton, where I boarded the United States Lines' "President Roosevelt" on October 28th. It was carrying my baggage and effects that had been loaded at its previous port of call – Hamburg.

Before the crossing the ship called at Cobh, and, as it departed, I kept looking at the receding Irish coast, poignantly conscious of taking my leave of Europe, in whose magnificent old culture I had been embedded.

We entered the outer harbor of New York in the early morning of Saturday, November 5th. The temperature was a welcoming 65 degrees, not unusual for a mild Indian-summer morning. I stood near the prow, looking at the magnificent 20th-century skyline ahead, dominated by the still new Empire State Building.

Eager to get my feet on my new homeland, I was one of the first to disembark – so promptly, in fact, that my passport contains no stamp or written entry documenting my arrival. It was about 8 a.m., and Lotti was nowhere to be seen. I put a nickel into a pay-phone and got her ex-German girl friend, with whom she was sharing the apartment and who told me that they hadn't expected me to be off the ship quite that early, but that Lotti was on her way. I hung around, and she arrived after a while. We hugged and proceeded to the apartment at 170 East 94th Street, 5D. Later that day she took me to 20 East 95th Street, off Fifth Avenue, a rooming house, where she had booked a room and where I would live until late November of 1939, when, in accordance with a much-delayed plan, I finally moved in with Lotti, after her friend began to share another apartment with her newly arrived mother.

Five days after my arrival I saw the headlines in the newspapers about the pogroms of the *"Kristallnacht"* in the country that I had had to leave scarcely four weeks before.

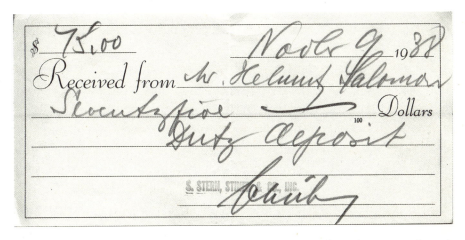

Check for 75 $ requested as security deposit for customs formalities carried out by S. Stern, Stiner & Co. in New York, issued on November 9th, 1938 – the day of the "Kristallnacht".

My mother had carefully, intelligently, and lovingly planned and doubtless also supervised an astonishingly large job of assembling and packing of effects, including some furniture, for my emigration, with every item and its location painstakingly listed on a number of handwritten slips of paper that I still have. The only remaining piece is that wooden cabinet with its glass-paneled door that came from my Hamburg bedroom.

As I settled into my one-room digs, I found a few things that gave special evidence of her solicitous thoughtfulness. For my shoes she had provided shoe trees, each of which she had conscientiously marked either R or L, apparently mistrusting my visual acuity even more than it deserved. I still use them. She had enclosed somewhere a small, stiff-covered copying book, containing fifty numbered sets of two pages, between any pair of which the loose piece of carbon paper was to be inserted; the inner edge of each top sheet was perforated. On the cover, on top of the printed word

Durchschreibbuch, she had written "Helmut" and underneath was her hand-written explanation: *"Das Buch bleibt zu Hause – Die Zettel bekommt der Bleicher mit."* (The book is kept at home – the [top] slips go along to the laundry.) I didn't use page no. 1, on the top of which she had written

Wäschebuch
The ...th of Novembre

My first visit to the laundry wasn't until a month after my arrival, by which time I had been working for two weeks and must have felt that I could afford to send out some laundry. Shirts cost 10 cents a piece, nightshirts 15 cents, handkerchiefs 2 cents, a pillow-case 3 cents. It seems that my financial constraints were such that I wore two shirts a week and did my underwear myself.

For an inexperienced young man barely twenty years old, whose active knowledge of English was still quite dismal, finding a job was a daunting undertaking. Though my father had solicited and collected many very respectable letters of recommendation for me from erstwhile business acquaintances with contacts in New York, all of which I followed up, it must have been apparent to the presidents, chairmen, etc. to whom I wrote, asking for an opportunity to present myself, that I was a green and rather tongue-tied immigrant youth, who was anything but God's gift to the still faltering economy.

One kindly addressee, a Mr. Rockey, president of an American firm called Chilean Nitrate Corporation, said that he regretted, like all the others, not being able to offer me any position, but that he would recommend me to his friend, Mr. Chalkley, the president of Philip Morris. Mr. Chalkley, also very nice, introduced me to Mr. Hanson, the vice-president for personnel, a thin, tallish, and very "WASPy" older man, who, apparently somewhat less than delighted to deal with this refugee boy, said that the best they might be able to do for me – at some later time – was the job of an office boy. He suggested in his dour way that I phone in the not too early future (say, six weeks).

That was that. I had played the cards that Vati had given me and for several days moped around in Lotti's apartment, while she, long having been fluent in English, was working at her secretarial job in the reasonably well-functioning office of immigrant stockbrokers. One day she came home with the news that she had heard of a job for me with a Mr. Bache, a name that I knew to be prominent in banking in those days. This man, however – also a refugee from Germany – was no banker, but a small-time importer and jobber of glass knickknacks, largely from Germany and Czechoslovakia. I went to be interviewed (mostly in German) by him in his small office at 225 Fifth Avenue, north of Madison Square Park. He offered me ten dollars – for a five-and-a-half-day week, which, though abysmal pay even in those days, was a 100 percent improvement for me, and I was delighted to take the job, two weeks after my arrival.

His agreement to have me work for him, however, was the happiest moment of my six months with him. The man was an exploiter and a slob; my most indelible memory of him is spitting the seeds on the stone floor as he ate an orange. As his sole employee I did everything for him – keeping his books, answering the phone when he was out, keeping the stock shelves in good order, taking care of his correspondence and billing, and cleaning up. The weekly ten dollars, with all deliberate frugality, didn't quite cover my expenses, and so I had to dig – minimally – into the savings my father had been able to pass along to me; after deduction of the Nazis' extortionate fees the generous sum of RM 60,000 had shrunk to roughly (1938) $ 2,000.

During my free times I tried conscientiously to improve my American English, by reading the paper – including the comics (so it wasn't The New York Times) – and occasionally going to the movies. When reading, I of course always had the dictionary handy; it was still an English-German dictionary – a help, though also a conceptual hindrance with its non-English definitions. It wasn't until some time later, when, following Lotti's suggestion, I read Margaret Mitchell's recently published *Gone With The Wind*, that the famous sweep of the narrative liberated me from that umbilical cord, and I remember reading heedlessly and with mounting excitement until I had finished the book at 3:00 a.m.

As time went on, I'd occasionally call Philip Morris, always to be told that nothing had come up. Finally, in June, after the kind Mr. Rockey's intercession on my behalf, they must have tired of my inquiries and I was told that they had an opening for an office boy. I informed Mr. Bache that I was leaving, proudly taking note of his dejection. The pay for my new job ($ 12), a 20 percent improvement, was just enough to cover my expenses including the five dollars a week for my room and even an occasional 10 cents for a malted milk, which was a new experience for me that I had come to love and whose disappearance I regret even now. Moreover, I was relieved of the expense of buying cigarettes, since there was a built-in perk for all employees, i.e. the periodic distribution of a carton of cigarettes. I had enjoyed occasional smoking since my adolescence, when my father, presumably to legitimate a practice I was bound to experiment with, offered me a cigarette. Inevitably I now became a heavy smoker, a habit I didn't shed for nearly two decades.

The office-boys – there were about half a dozen of them – mostly came from Irish-immigrant families; the names that come to mind are Ray McNabb, Bob Dyer, and Jimmy Deegan; the latter was a poet, getting rejections from the magazines to which he submitted his poems. He favored *The New Yorker*, because, as he said, he admired its stylish rejection slips. Our "office" in the rear of the executive floor at 119 Fifth Avenue (at East 19th Street) was the narrow and window-less stock room, where we would sit on unopened cardboard containers and wait to be assigned jobs by Mr. Hough, our overseer, who received calls for our services at his desk outside. There often were long waits, during which I was introduced to the excitement of poker – literally penny-ante. The boys were quite decent to me, considering that I was a marked curiosity. They would razz me occasionally about my un-New-Yorkish ways and my awkward English. Bob Dyer claimed that one could always tell my feelings, since my eyes, presumably unlike those of most Americans, gave away my reactions to what others said.

It was primarily in that stock room that in the course of about six months I finally learned to become an English speaker, though not without at least one contingent misadventure, when I was given verbal instructions to deliver an unaddressed envelope at some office. I thought I had understood, but wasn't quite sure. Not wanting to ask, I proceeded to take it to an incorrect address. My ineptitude was duly and embarrassingly noted on my return and I was ignominiously sent out to retrieve and redeliver the material.

I thought that surely that would be the end of my incipient career, but they were good to me and kept me on. After a while I became better able to justify their confidence; the accuracy, speed, efficiency, and commitment of my services began to be noticed, and sometime in 1940 I was transferred to clerical work in the Traffic and Export Departments. The young fellow I was assigned to work with was expected to leave after a while, and I was designated in due course to take over his job. And so I had a desk of my own, working for two bosses – the Traffic Manager (a very nice, burly man of Scandinavian background, whose job was to oversee domestic shipping) and the Export Manager, who was a Vice-President and who after some time commended me informally for being capable enough for him to rely on me. My parents were pleased and relieved that I had an adequately paid job, which, as a matter of fact, I owed to my father's efforts on my behalf. They had some time ago given up the useless and demoralizing burden of the house[16] and moved into the ground floor of the neighboring house at no. 29, from which they could look at their former garden, where I remember Vati, just a few years before, reading and trying to come to terms with Oswald Spengler's *Der Untergang des Abendlandes* (The Demise of the West), a complex, difficult, and gloomy book.

By that time Hitler's war was well into its second year. It had left its mark on my English family, who had yet to obtain their British citizenship. Franz was interned in mid-1940 as an enemy alien and was sent to a camp on the Isle of Man for men of that ilk, leaving Hildi and Inge in greater isolation and in a rather precarious financial situation. In due course Hildi found out that appeals to one's Member of Parliament were sometimes successful in getting such obvious misclassifications repealed and their victims released. Those procedures tended to take time, however, and Franz, finally giving in to hopeless impatience, did what was in his power to be sprung from internment: he volunteered for the Army. The next day Hildi received word from her MP that it would be possible to release Franz from his internment, but, as the saying goes, the die was cast. He joined his family for occasional furloughs. Inge, who certainly, together with her mother, had the most stressful wartime life of the younger component of our family, later told me that for a major part of his army career Franz functioned as interpreter at a prisoner-of-war camp, apparently with great success, since the inmates in his charge, upon his release in June of 1945, presented him with a concert (Schubert Lieder, etc.) in his honor.

Home of the Salomon Family, St. Benediktstraße 27, Hamburg-Harvestehude

Lucia Salomon, née Königswerther (ca. 1938)

Paul Salomon (ca. 1938)

← *Helmut Salomon (ca. 1942)*

← *Helmut Salomon (ca. 1928)*

Helmut Salomon with his graduating class, c. October 1936, in front of the main entrance of the Johanneum, with principal teacher Dr. Ax. The picture was taken a few months before graduation, since several students, facing a military draft in the fall of 1936, had to have an early "emergency graduation."

– *Front row, from the left: Salomon, von Puttkamer, Ax*
– *Second row, from the left: Hewicker, Overweg (behind von Puttkamer and Ax)*
– *Second row, from the right: Andreae, Pump*
– *Above Puttkamer: Palm*
– *Above Ax: Laun*
– *Above Pump: Brandis*
  To the left and behind Brandis: Hadamczik

Paul Salomon, Franz Friedlaender, Lucie Salomon,
Inge Friedlaender and Helmut Salomon on the terrace St. Benediktstraße
(probably 1937)

Helmut Salomon's Bedroom

Paul Salomon was deprived of the free use of his assets: Schedule of assets and monthly expenses, in accordance with the regulations in the Security Ordinance ("Sicherungsanordnung"), 16 September, 1939

THE PARENTS' LIFE AND DEATH

Like a typical German youth I asked my father in a letter about a year after my emigration whether he might write an overview of his life and thinking; I'm sure the word *Weltanschauung* had a prominent place in my request. Sensibly he complied with the following thoughtful memoir – like him, totally honest and honorable, lucid and rational. (The translation of Mutti's typescript was made by my sister Lotti for her husband.)

My early-childhood memories are interwoven with the images of the rooms in which my family lived at the time. These images are most vivid in my mind's eye: the parlor with its walnut furniture and green upholstery; the living room with its table covered by a colorfully bordered cloth that had a special appeal for me; the simple bedroom of my parents, which at that time was shared by my youngest sister, and finally the room for the four oldest children. This room was like a Jack-of-all-trades; it was here that we ate our meals; after dinner my parents would either read the paper or a book, and this was where the children worked and played. Many a bitter pillow fight took place in that room! – Modern means of sanitation, which nowadays are taken for granted, were by no means common in those days, since, after all, this was only the early seventies of the 19th century. The toilet was outside the apartment – practically "at the end of the world." We were able to reach it only through a long corridor. The human refuse was collected in a container in the courtyard, which was periodically siphoned through a hose the thickness of a man's arm, out of the house into a wagon, which was appropriately called "dung wagon," around which everyone made wide detours. –

We lived on the third floor, and the staircase had no landings. Our greatest thrill was to slide down the banister, the faster the better; youth knows no danger.

My memories of my father – except in my very early youth – are mostly those of a man worried how to make ends meet. He was a diligent and intelligent man, who only a few years before his death was able to live without those worries. He came from a relatively modest background and, in accordance with the customs of the times, went into apprenticeship at the age of 13. After several years of learning the trade he opened a dry goods store with his brother as partner. The business soon prospered, and at the age of 35 he married. My mother was good-looking, had had an excellent education and had an active mind. In addition, she brought along a handsome dowry, which was used to expand the business. The money went down the drain, because the business gradually faltered, partly because Mother's ambition to educate the children properly put too much pressure on the financial state of the business. Those are sad memories of my young life – the shop without customers, my father's perpetually worried expression, and my furtive glances into the daily ledger. I was a quiet boy who thought a great deal, and it didn't take much to guess what the end result would be. And so the collapse came. Bankruptcy was a traumatic experience, and I looked at this disaster as something shameful. I tried to avoid my classmates, but they probably didn't even know what had happened.

We were what is commonly called gifted children, and our ambitious mother was elated to have four children at the head of their class. In my case it was a short-lived triumph, because I soon became lazy and scatterbrained and had trouble keeping up with the class. Doubtless it would have been better if my parents had withdrawn me from school at the time. Thanks to my mother's ambition and my father's sacrifices I was finally able to complete my education at the *Gymnasium*. Towards the end of my school years I finally did better and was able to do adequate work in some subjects. Math, however, was a nightmare, and the memories of this course have haunted me even into mature manhood. There also was anti-semitism that cast a further shadow upon my youth.

My brother and I were the first children of Jewish parents who attended the *Stadtgymnasium* (public high school) in Halle. The principal was a fine person, who has had my lifelong admiration. He was an idealist, who was completely free of prejudices and who had had to pay for his patriotism with the loss of a leg in the war of 1850. In school the noisy pupils were always forewarned of his coming because of the loud stomping of his wooden leg on the floor. The faculty was not outstanding and in many cases old-fashioned, though generally broadminded in their attitude to Jews. Not so the classmates, particularly those from the middle classes. Our absence from the lectures on religion sharply accentuated the difference. This period was usually scheduled as the first one of the day, and I therefore had the advantage of sleeping an extra hour twice a week, but the tremendous disadvantage that I always had to wait in front of the closed door, until the teacher had left the classroom. I was depressed by the fact that I was not the same as the rest of the children and this contributed to my feeling of inferiority. Throughout my life I worked in vain to overcome this complex, which was intensified during military service and later abated with professional success. Today I no longer have any complexes; instead, my inferiority is officially certified.

But I return to the subject of my school. My mathematics teacher is the one I remember most vividly, and yet I learned the least in his class and was a nonentity in his eyes. He expended a great deal of effort on me for a considerable length of time; when finally, however, he realized that I was a hopeless case, he treated me with disdain. He just could not understand how anyone could be that disinterested in mathematics and interpreted my apathy as bad intention; alas, he didn't know that I really didn't understand the subject! His remarks on my exam papers bore ample witness to his attitude. On the rare occasions that I managed to do well in a test he assumed that I must have cheated. I did recognize even then, however, that this was a true teacher, committed to teaching his pupils. I am humbly grateful to him for his generosity in giving me a "pass" in Math and Physics upon graduation; his commentary was a masterpiece of half concealing and half revealing the fact that I really knew nothing in either subject.

With foreign languages I had fewer difficulties, being sustained by a quick and sure memory; but here, too, my written work caused my teachers the expenditure of much red ink. Greek was taught by three teachers. The first – a toothless, mumbling old man – was an emeritus university professor, the second resembled the Zeus of Otricoli, whose replica looked down in Olympic calm upon us in our classroom, and the third bore a resemblance to Bacchus, as depicted by Hauff in his *Phantasies in the Bremen Rathskeller*. The latter took a liking to me and, though he had caused me not to be promoted from the eighth grade, made me one of his "inner circle", thus allowing me to participate in a weekly meeting in his apartment. It was considered a privilege bestowed only on special students. The evenings were devoted to reading the Greek classics, much of which would have escaped us without his guidance. Of course, young people being what they are, we would have preferred to be outside, but in retrospect I have fond memories of those evenings.

My family's attitude towards our religion and the instruction we were given is a significant topic. Both my parents were raised in the Jewish faith and fully adhered to it, though more out of habit than true religious conviction. Nevertheless, the two principal Jewish holidays were observed in the strictest manner. The business was closed, the children did not attend school, but joined the parents in going to the synagogue, and we even fasted on Yom Kippur. Those visits to the temple caused in me a feeling of humiliation that it didn't take me long to recognize. The house of worship was located in a hidden part of the city; the approach and entrance of the worshippers was always scrutinized by a line of curious spectators. Inside, the visitors were greeted by dank and stuffy air; on High Holy Days the congregants left the house of worship only at night. I was repelled by the Hebrew prayers, which I couldn't understand, by customs alien to me in their Oriental origin, and, last not least, by the apparent indifference of the congregants. Young as I was, I apparently sensed that religion seemed well served by simply remaining at the services for the required time. These experiences have been decisive for me with respect to religion in general. Moreover, we had no religious instruction whatsoever until the proper time for Bar Mitzvah, which, in accordance with old ritual, took place at the age of thirteen. But what did this instruction consist of? I learned sufficient Hebrew to be able to read – but not to understand, so that I could recite a modest piece from the Torah. Once I had done so, religious instruction again stopped for the remainder of my school career, except for the last three months before graduation. My good old principal decided that my religious education was insufficient for graduation and demanded written confirmation from the Rabbi, attesting to my religious instruction and moral maturity. I had no choice but to comply with that requirement. Since I was already estranged from the Jewish faith – I was almost 19 years old – the Rabbi, with exceptional sensitivity, gave me permission to participate in a number of lectures on Jewish history, since I had always been interested in history. This ended religious instruction once and for all; it is therefore hardly surprising that throughout my life I have remained a secular outsider in matters of faith. I did not deny the existence of God, but never have I been able to embrace the concept of total Goodness and Justice. Our experience of recent years seems to support my belief that for any such Higher Being the fate of the individual must remain inconsequential and that therefore all prayers, stammered in hope and despair, will remain unanswered. Prayers serve merely as tranquilizer for a hopeful and tormented soul, but have no prospect of fulfillment.

I have always looked upon faith as a product of both fear and hope; it certainly seems to me that the religions of primitive tribes are based on this amalgam. As mankind advanced spiritually and intellectually, it seems that a God who was to be honored was to become more distant. Watching the rituals of worship has always made me feel as if man had shaped God after his image rather than the opposite. Thus, religious rites have always either bored me or had the effect of being theatrical; I preferred the latter result as being more effective. This may help to explain the particular strength of Catholicism. In spite of my negative approach to religion I have always recognized the enormous creative power of true and pure faith; true believers have always had my respect and even envy.

My circle of friends was limited during my childhood and school years and – casting a glance at later times – has always remained so, because of the way youthful experiences shaped my particular attitudes. All in all, I have always led a more or less encapsulated life. The half dozen friends I had in school were soon lost, as we scattered in different directions in preparations for our various professional futures. My career led me to the world of business, for which I cannot claim to have had any particular inclination or talent. On the contrary, I would have much preferred to follow the traditional route to college, like my brother and my schoolmates. I turned out to be the first graduate of the Gymnasium not to go to college, because my parents' financial circumstances were insufficient and besides I somehow felt that basically I was not of the caliber to pursue a professional career. And so I went into business, neither willingly nor unwillingly, but regretting the necessity of wasting my good humanistic education. Later it turned out that it had not been a total loss. While it was of no advantage to me in my day-to-day business life, I have adhered to the belief that a humanistic education is invaluable, as long as it remains unweakened by petty philological issues. Until a few years ago the modern *Gymnasium* has fulfilled my views and ideals; lately it has moved into particular directions that I cannot understand and which I believe will prove harmful in the long run.

During the first months of my apprenticeship I had to contend with the conceit induced by my education, an attitude that unfortunately was supported by my family, with the exception of my eldest sister, who was a sensible girl and swept away all that silliness with her lapidary remark, "Don't turn the silly boy's head!" I've always remained grateful to her. Gradually I realized that knowledge and education alone are not decisive, but must be accompanied by character and secure ability. In later years, when I had to make decisions on the assignment of people, I based my determinations on my confidence in their character and ability, regardless of their social background and education.

My training in a provincial bank turned out to be extremely inadequate; much of my apprenticeship was wasted with petty manual work. This taught me next to nothing. Finally, after three long years, I finished my apprenticeship and actually had learned very little. To my great surprise a bank in Hamburg was willing to give me a chance. Even in later years I was never able to back up my ability with a feeling of total security; I did try to fill the gaps, but much remained undone, and even after I had reached a responsible position I often had to rely on others, when I myself should have made sure. I was very much aware of this weakness, because my principle was "Deceive no one, least of all yourself." In accordance with Moltke's saying that "The capable are entitled to good fortune" and in view of my awareness of my inadequacy I should have been condemned to a life of failure. However, the opposite came to pass; I was lucky, again and again. Something must be wrong here, but evidently others were even dumber than I.

Music was of some importance in my parents' home, although my mother – unless my memory fails me – was quite unmusical. I never heard her sing, but my father loved music and had a very good ear for it. Unfortunately circumstances did not permit him to develop his dormant talents. Piano lessons were considered an essential part of our general education and so my two older sisters and my older brother, as well as my younger sister in later years, had lessons; none of them advanced beyond average ability. I refused to take lessons, and I suspect my parents were not too unhappy, since it meant saving money. Years later I was sorry that I had made that decision, as it turned out that I was not nearly as unmusical as I had tried to convince myself and others. My two older sisters had lovely voices – alto and soprano – and sang diligently and beautifully at home. They belonged to a large choral society, where they sang with great enthusiasm. Because of their singing I gained a thorough knowledge of the Lieder repertoire and choral works. As the years went by and I attended concerts, this knowledge contributed greatly to my enjoyment of music. Nevertheless, my relation to music as well as to all other arts has always remained primitive, since I had no training in any of the arts. But I felt the need to balance my sometimes tedious business life with one or another of the arts. I didn't ask for much, since my understanding was limited. It is therefore easy to see why I would reject what would produce ecstatic reactions in others. My love has always gone to Mozart, whose grace and clarity continued to delight me, and only secondarily to Beethoven. Complexity and, especially, mysticism were abhorrent to me. I have never concealed the fact that I basically disliked Wagner, even though admittedly he often stirred my enthusiasm. This was partly due to his choice of material and partly to the at times insufferable noisiness of his music. It seems that Mozart and Wagner represent clearly the difference between Northern Germany and old Austria: effortless grace – even in tragedy – on the one hand, and on the other a powerful and often nearly brutal assault on the listener's nerves. Needless to say there is a political parallel. However, these are only the impressions of an uneducated layman.

I had similar reactions to paintings. Even the most famous masterworks left me cold, if I couldn't understand them immediately or succumb to the beauty of their colors. I had never been able to draw or paint, and since in accordance with the principle of opposites one appreciates most what one lacks, clean draftsmanship was for me always the fundamental element in my perception of a painting. Therefore I always admired Menzel and have totally rejected the color orgies of the last two decades. If the exhibits of "Degenerate Art" that swept Germany recently had not served other purposes, I could wholeheartedly have subscribed to the extermination of unwholesome art and to promote healthy art perception.

My relations to my sisters and brother were good, apart from the usual childhood fights. My brother was my mother's pride and joy, because he was a far better student than I. He sometimes got in my way, because, knowing my classmates, he inevitably heard of my frequent failures in school. But we got along well; I was the more tolerant one in those days. My two older sisters – not much older than I – had to witness the financial collapse of our family in their mature youth. They witnessed the daily worries at an early age and were left without friends. There just wasn't enough money for the girls' education, in addition to that of the boys. The tedious embroidering of handkerchiefs brought in no more than a meager amount of pocket money. Years later my eldest sister broke with all prejudices and decided to take a job in an office. Her life suddenly had meaning and her successful work brought her fulfillment. My youngest sister decided not to wait that long and she, too, took a job, which gave her great satisfaction. As soon as I was financially able, I saw to it that my middle sister received training as a singing teacher. For many years she supported herself in this profession, which gave her great satisfaction. I was happy to be able to give her this fulfillment and I was also happy that my brother, who had just established himself as a physician, and I managed to pay off my father's creditors. It took us four long years to settle the debts, but we were proud of this accomplishment. (In later years, when money was no longer a problem, I continued to assist my mother and sisters; then there was no reason for pride, since no financial effort was involved.) In view of these financial obligations, it was difficult for me to accumulate capital; this in turn handicapped me in socializing with people potentially helpful in my professional career and thus slowed its progress. In later fateful times my memories of those years were to be decisive in my refusal to leave Germany to join our children, who have escaped just in time. In my overbearing stubbornness I rejected any thought of emigration time and time again, and I therefore would consider it foolhardy today perhaps to rob our children of the modest comfort they enjoy now and put at risk the possibility of professional advance, merely in order that we may exist a little longer. It pains me that I have enmeshed my loyal wife and partner in this fate; she fully shares my views, however.

During my life I came to recognize the value of the bonds holding siblings together; whatever money I was able to give was returned to me two- and three-fold in love and gratitude. After finishing my apprenticeship I stayed at the bank another six months for a monthly salary of RM 60 – and subsequently was in military service for one year. Nothing noteworthy happened during this period, except that physically and mentally I survived it well. Those of us, including Jews, who were well-educated were chosen to be trained as reserve officers. Needless to say that Jewish young men only rarely made the grade, but what this training did for us was to teach us how to be in command; we learned not only to obey, but also to command, both of which are important skills in life; the latter is the more difficult one.

The day after my military discharge I ventured forth to Hamburg – my new home. Railroad connections were quite poor in those days, and the train carrying me and my fate to Hamburg took about ten hours and stopped at almost every shack, as if to say, "Good things take time." My ideas of the future were rather hazy; I wasn't too confident of my abilities, but nevertheless had, since the arrival of the letter with its offer of employment, dreamed of success in the strange big city. Little did I anticipate that I would spend my entire life there; the only way I mused this would be possible was if I married the daughter of a city senator and therefore would have the door opened for me to become a "royal merchant." In my youthful innocence – I was then 24 years old – I considered such an event entirely possible. Reality turned out to be different, and it took a very long time to ascend the long ladder of success. Nonetheless, the beginning seemed to justify my dreams. My superiors recognized that I wanted to get ahead and that I was of a more serious mind than most of my colleagues; to my surprise they advanced me so quickly that I thought I had reached the first step on the ladder to success, i.e. proxy (the right to sign), when a big corporation collapsed, to which my bank had committed itself with irresponsibly large loans. My hopes were dashed. The manager who thought well of me was dismissed and was replaced by a tight bureaucrat who liked to make money, but had no desire to see anybody else do so. My whole work had to start again from scratch; it took another three long years to reach what I had thought to be on the point of accomplishing. I consider those three years the most difficult of my life; if it hadn't been for the challenges created by the never-ending financial difficulties in Halle, I doubt that I would have stayed with the job, as I saw no possibility for advancement. My hands were tied: however; as it turned out, it was my good fortune. When I reached the position of *Prokurist* (deputy director), I was thirty years old. I had no more dreams; my daily work had squashed them. Nonetheless it was a fact that I was beginning to be respected in the bank and elsewhere for my ability and that, indeed, I had a position of modest importance. It wasn't undeserved; I knew nothing apart from the bank and my work, I was striving hard to gain more knowledge, and in a way began to be the sort of superior to those working under me who is respected, but not loved. I must add that it was most helpful to me that I had a modest knowledge of foreign languages. During my apprenticeship I had been working on my French and English; my claim to fluency in those languages had been instrumental in getting me the job in Hamburg. I was shaking in my boots whenever I thought of my approaching debut as linguist, and, indeed, I could have been in trouble if the bank at that time had had extensive foreign correspondence and if indeed the others hadn't known even less than I did. In view of many years' experience I consider knowledge – I mean thorough knowledge – of foreign languages an absolutely essential tool for achieving success in business, in addition to the necessary specialized professional education. Ordinarily, basic knowledge must be unexceptionable in any business or profession, at least for those who start at the bottom. To be sure, there are cases in business when born leaders achieve a high degree of success without thorough knowledge of details; still, these are exceptions. The best boss will always be the one who is able to carry out even the smallest job and has thorough knowledge of the business.

It took me twelve years to advance from *Prokurist* to the position of Assistant Director (or Manager). Those were long years and I was dissatisfied with my rate of progress. Several times I made the attempt to leave Germany and try my luck abroad. Twice negotiations progressed to a point where it was up to me to accept the quite satisfactory conditions of my prospective employers. One job would have been in one of the Russian provinces on the Baltic Sea and the other with a smaller bank in Guatemala that had special connections with Hamburg. Both jobs fell through due to my excessive demands based on my concerns for adequate security. Perhaps this was my good fortune, as it turned out that neither job developed into what I had been led to believe during the negotiations. Moreover, it was unlikely that I would have been young enough to adjust to such a drastic change. Thus, I stayed where I was, made some more – but not enough – money, advanced quite slowly and was in a rut. I started to become indifferent and resigned myself to a career of mediocrity.

During all those years the thought of marriage had not entered my mind. I wouldn't have dared to think of taking such a step because of my responsibilities for voluntary contributions to the family, which precluded any sizable accumulation of capital. Moreover, whatever capital I had, had been lost by speculation. This calamity taught me a lesson; expensive as it was, it was not in vain. From it I learned never to exceed my ability and responsibilities, and I never again experienced similar difficulties, although my professional daily contact with the stock exchange offered ample opportunities. Rather, I developed an attitude of calm judiciousness and strict restraint that caused my income to increase substantially. Apart from economic reasons, I perhaps rejected any thought of marriage because of shyness and an exaggerated feeling of responsibility. All those years had encapsulated me to a point where, aside from a few old friends, I saw hardly anyone. Besides, I found conventional social contacts mostly boring, and for the life of me I couldn't imagine what a girl would see in me. But then, at age 38 1/2, I met the young woman who was to become my loyal and loving partner during the second epoch of my life. Much to my surprise I managed to overcome seemingly insurmountable difficulties and so I abandoned all scruples. It was my great good fortune that the woman who shared my life was not only the loving wife, but also the honest, energetic, and intelligent companion I needed. From the start our marriage was good and will remain so until the end of our days.

Marriage meant new responsibilities and released new energies in me; nonetheless it took another three years until I reached the position of assistant manager. In the meantime we had become parents. We moved from our first modest apartment to a somewhat larger one, 96 stairs up! In those days I was in very good physical condition and many a time I dashed past our door and landed up in the attic. (In due course I lost some of this exuberance; thirty years have come and gone since those days.) We spent some of our happiest years in that apartment; our little daughter was a source of joy for us, and my career was finally on the upswing. Business was not always easy; a considerable economic and financial crisis had shaken business life in Hamburg. Moreover, there were indications that Germany's poor foreign policy would some day result in a clash with her old enemies. It took another seven years until war broke out, but the old optimism was gone. Yet, nobody could envisage the extent of the disaster to come, and thus we spent those years calmly and happily.

Two years before the outbreak of the war – we were then expecting our second child – we decided to move once again. As I now was in a better financial position, I wanted something more ostentatious, and we therefore chose a so-called upper-class apartment with all modern conveniences. I don't know the reason – perhaps the disastrous war years, or the postwar period, or whatever else – the fact is that we were no happier in that apartment nor, for that matter, in the house we purchased twelve years later than in our "tower apartment." Perhaps we were never again as happy. I'll skim over the effects of war and their political consequences; the facts are well-known. One result of the war that affected us the most was the German inflation, which climaxed in November 1923, five years after the end of the war and the Kaiser's abdication. It brought with it the total annihilation of the German currency in the international market. At the beginning of this disastrous process no one was fully aware of what was going on; after the collapse the consequences were easily foreseen. In my case it meant the almost total loss of earned capital, my wife's dowry and her inheritance. In short, it meant that a new start had to be made. But the miracle happened: I succeeded. Meanwhile I had been elected to the directorate of the Hamburg branch of the Dresdner Bank; my income had risen considerably, and I managed to add to it in large measure during the feverish period of reconstruction between 1924 and 1930, erroneously regarded as flourishing.

Meanwhile there had been changes in the family. The first one to leave us was my father, who died in 1901 after a lengthy illness. The next to die was my father-in-law, to be followed in 1913, shortly after our second daughter was born, by my mother-in-law, whom I admired greatly. And in December 1918, in the midst of military collapse and revolution, we became the parents of a son. My mother, whose last years I was happily able to make unworried, left us in 1926. She was full of pride, knowing that both her sons had become owners of private homes. (What a blessing that she is not here now to see that this ownership has now been taken from us.) Last, not least, my sister-in-law passed away the previous year. We must consider it a blessing, because she didn't have to witness the scattering of the large and wealthy family. Now everyone is gone with the wind; we, too, have had to bid farewell to our three children, granddaughter, and son-in law. Theirs is a strange new world, their future uncertain.

The false prosperity of 1924–1930 was succeeded in 1931 by an international financial and economic crisis. As they had in the period of inflation, nations all over the world placed blind confidence and speculative hope in Germany and lent huge sums of money, which were irretrievably lost. After the currency reforms, the international banking world had heedlessly made available huge amounts in Pounds and Dollars as short-term loans, which the German banks accepted; inevitably this led to catastrophe. These amounts – at a high interest rate – could only have been useful, if there had been security against sudden withdrawal. Though there was no such security, the German banks proceeded to immobilize these amounts by in turn lending them to industry. When the forerunner of the world crisis – the collapse of the American stock market – made cautious money lenders stop and take a good hard look, the withdrawals began. In 1931 the calls for withdrawals became panicky. Naturally, payments could not be made. This resulted in the collapse of many industrial enterprises and banks. My bank, too, had to undergo complete reorganization. It was during this period that I retired. Undoubtedly the events of this economic period have contributed to the growing anti-semitism in Germany, although of course Jews and Christians alike had made the same mistakes. I don't resent the end of my business life – after all, it came at an advanced age – but I am hurt by the disloyalty of those with whom I have had friendly relations for many years. This also applies to the bank, which I served to the best of my ability for forty-four years.

Before I close this short and sketchy summary of my life, I would like to add a few remarks regarding our children and their education. Being far apart in age as they are creates problems for parents as well as children. Normal age differences facilitate the upbringing and lessen the possibility of friction among the siblings. At the time our second child was born, the eldest was seven years old, and the youngest was again five years and three quarters younger than the middle one. It is hardly surprising, therefore, that, as the children grew up, arguments and friction were common occurrences. The eldest wanted to guide, the younger girl rejected such attempts, and this conflict was intensified by totally different temperaments. We frequently worried about these discords, particularly since we apparently were unable to bring the two temperaments into balance. Both girls, however, always had a wonderful relationship with their brother. Our elder daughter was like a second mother, who guided him with loving and conscientious loyalty. She contributed in no small amount to his development. Aside from those occasional worries we derived nothing but joy from raising our children. All were healthy and of normal intelligence and graduated from school without undue difficulty, in fact quite easily in the cases of Nos. 1 and 3. Our middle child for some years seemed headed towards the same kind of school career as her father, but eventually pulled herself together and graduated satisfactorily. My primary principle in raising children was training them to be truthful. I remember only too well how, as a child, I occasionally succumbed to using the tool of the weak: lying. I tried to teach my children how futile a folly this was. To this principle I adhered strictly. Once our eldest earned herself a solid spanking, because, being fanatically truthful, she had doubted the veracity of what I had just said. Strictly speaking, she was right, and I suspect that subconsciously I took it out on her, remembering my earlier days of occasional lying. In other respects I tried to give my children as much freedom as possible, particularly not to put undue pressure on them regarding their scholastic success, in that respect I had no particular ambition. I was satisfied if they did their work– as they got older, however, I emphasized thoroughness, and I wasn't always popular, when it came to quizzing them for tests.

I was unable to introduce my children into the joys of art appreciation, since I didn't know enough about it, but I did manage to awaken the pleasure in the beauties of nature. Over and over I urged them to be aware of the beauty of the world and the joy of the moment and not to complain if good things came to an end. I always had a streak of Cassandra in me! – I was able to exercise some influence and guidance when listening to their piano playing. I stressed the necessity of technical flawlessness, since I felt that this was essential to the enjoyment of music. I detested any glossing over mistakes; any performer guilty of such a habit is comparable to the reader of a foreign language, skimming over words he doesn't know and too lazy to use a dictionary.

This then, is the end of my story. I have omitted details of my life in later years; they are unimportant in the life of an average individual. It is also futile to talk about our recent years and the burden we have had to bear and will have to continue to endure in increased intensity. In my opinion there is no longer any chance of extricating ourselves from the degrading situation in which we have become enmeshed undeservedly. All we can do is to resign ourselves and await the end with composure.

Our children have been in foreign lands for years; their letters alone give meaning to our empty lives. We will not see them again, but cling to the hope that they have found happiness in their new homelands.

On the 15th of July, 1939, my father had written the following polite, but remarkably outspoken letter to an acquaintance (my translation):

My dear Doctor,
To my great regret I gather from your letter, which arrived yesterday, that you have found little reason to be satisfied with your life since your return to the U.S.A., and so I first of all express my wish for speedy improvement. Nevertheless we

were delighted to receive your letter because of your positive words regarding our children, as well as your unchanged friendly disposition towards us – a disposition we generally no longer encounter here. […] I am forced to conclude that your information as to what has befallen us since November *[Kristallnacht]* is highly insufficient. Lying sleeplessly in bed last night and thinking of you and your letter, I kept remembering Schiller's words:

Wohl dem, der frei von Schuld und Fehle
Bewahrt die kindlich reine Seele!

Bless him who, free of guilt's and error's toll,
Preserves his childlike purity of soul!

You know my entirely objective view of what is going on, including my recognition of what has been achieved in foreign policy; but when I think of everything we here have had to bear in silence, I can well understand your former friend's decision [presumably to emigrate]. I won't dwell on material things – though, to be sure, the imposition of monetary penalty for a stupidity not committed by us [the assassination leading to the *Kristallnacht*], the surrender of the house, the prohibition of car ownership and of all entertainments, including even movies and sports events, are not easy to bear; but the daily abuse in the papers and the public defamation are truly unbearable for anyone not burdened by guilt. And in addition there is the complete, the absolute hopelessness with respect to the future! . . . Even the highest goal is no justification for every expedient. […]

My mother wrote the following letter (September 9th–10th, 1941) to Lotti and me in New York:[17]

Dear Children,

I added to the last letter that I would write during the week, but I was so busy that I had no time, we collected pears and they require a lot of work, otherwise, if you leave them untouched for a while, they rot. We gave away a lot and everybody was happy, because there is very little fruit at the moment. Just now Frau Seebach is on vacation. One evening I was dead tired, which is always proof that I cannot do too much any more. – Since yesterday new regulations have come into effect, which make life almost impossible, yesterday the doorbell rang the whole day, if we still had our telephone, it would have gone all day. But we cannot advise or help anybody. One's own problem is enough! It takes a lot to be so quiet, but nobody will notice anything with me, I don't know myself how I acquired this calmness. But again and again: Since you, dear Lo, came to the decision to leave and I said, "One has to become hard and cold to stand all this," I succeeded to retain my calm. – This is an unpleasant beginning of a letter! – I still want to answer your letter, Lo, of August 18, which you wrote immediately after your return – quite an accomplishment, since you came back the night before so late. How wonderful that you both enjoyed your vacation so much, I hope you will feel the recreation for a long time, congratulations on your tennis successes. I am always glad when I hear that from you, Lo and Hilde, not only is it good as far as sport and health is concerned, but very often it is a jumping board for relations and social success. If I only knew whether Hildi also plays. The former players here had little success in the tournaments, they are not much good. I still follow the reports, but there are not many big tournaments any more. Remember the times when we went to the big international tournaments, even in the private loge!! – In your next letter, Lo, we shall probably hear what you got as prize. And you, Helmut, what you got for your overtime, and whether the new salary has been fixed yet. I always said, I still wanted to see you on the road to success and that you, Lo, would find a decent and clever husband, let us hope that fate has this still in store for you. As far as HFs[18] are concerned, we hope that we shall not have to worry too much any more, they will, I hope, master their life. It will be difficult for you to have everything as we had it and you had it with us, it is beautiful and wonderful if one has it, but it is not necessary for happiness. Va's old friend Cornelius [von Berenberg-Gossler], you know, was here this morning with a bunch of flowers, and the whole family is charming. – In the meantime we celebrated Paula M.'s birthday, I expect your congratulations will arrive this week, we were there in the afternoon, then the whole atmosphere was still a happier one and all her friends were so nice to her, then she is always happy, she also had a report from Bubi, he is well. Annemie's letter had not yet arrived either. Her old maid Grete came with her daughter in the morning and brought coffee and cake so that she would not have to eat her breakfast alone, she is wonderful. All the old servants prove that there are still people in the world who remember what we were and how we were!! – The two sisters Brosius [seamstresses] are also lovely people. It seems that Kurtchen's parents are away, we could not reach them, they wanted to see their sons, but did not know yet when. They get our frigidaire so that they can think of us every day, it is very useful.

Sep. 10. Last night Kurtchen's parents [Laun] came, they are not away, they are, as usual, wonderful. We talked about everything, they of course do not share our opinion, although they understand everything. I just turned on the electric stove, it's been very cold since a few days, that was a crazy summer. I am so glad, Lo, that you decided to keep the apartment, you will find someone who likes to share the apartment with you, only you will have to put down a few things in writing, which was not necessary with Elle. Let us hope the best for all, maybe it doesn't have to be yet and you and Helmut can stay together for a while. I am glad that Stern lets you do such important things [in the office] as make the inventory of the customers' securities. I am sure, if M. would not be, you would even be further. Well, we have to be satisfied, but, above all, that we are fortunate enough to have decent children, who can master life. I hope you will all stay healthy and you will always stick together, one day HF's will read this, too. [...] You have enough friends and people who can advise you. I wish

Truderichs[18] all the best for the new apartment, they haven't written for a long time. We shall try to send you a few books for Christmas, but it is so difficult to find the right thing, and besides I don't think that much time is left for reading, maybe in later years.

I hope that you will always be very well, please write frequently to HFs. Regards and love to everybody, and you be embraced by

Yours,
MU
We had news from HFs yesterday, dated June 5.

Letter from Lucie Salomon to Ferdinand Bloch-Bauer[19] in Zurich (September 14th, 1941).

Lieber Onkel Ferdinand!
Ich habe Dir noch für Deinen letzten Brief – nein es war eine Karte, die Du kurz nach Deiner Rückkehr aus Zürich geschrieben hast, zu danken. – Ich freue mich, dass Du ein bisschen Erholung und Abwechslung gehabt hast. – Hoffentlich bleibt Dir die körperliche und geistige Frische noch lange erhalten. – Von uns kann ich Dir nur sagen, wir sind am Ende unserer Kräfte, es ist zu viel wieder, was in den letzten Wochen auf uns eingestürmt ist und noch einstürmt. Ich nehme an, dass Du von allem unterrichtet bist. – Wir haben lange tapfer stand gehalten, aber es gibt eben Dinge über die man nicht hinweg kommen kann, wenigstens wir nicht! – Ich glaube gar nicht, dass Du wirklich genau im Bilde bist, welche Stellung Paul hier hatte, und was er für eine geachtete und geschätzte Persönlichkeit war. – Wenn er das liest, wird er in seiner Bescheidenheit wieder sagen, „was für ein Unsinn!!" – Aber wie anerkannt und geschätzt Paul hier war, das beweisen auch heute noch Freunde, die trotz allem treu zu ihm halten. Wir haben ein glückliches Leben bis 33 geführt, und können darüber froh sein, dass unsere Kinder vor der schlimmsten Zeit herausgekommen sind, und Fuß fassen konnten, hoffentlich werden sie weiter vorwärts kommen, und auch ihr Leben wird von Glück und nicht allzu viel Sorgen begleitet sein. Ich hoffe es auch heute für Hilde, Franz und Inge! – Helmut steckt wahrscheinlich jetzt schon in der Uniform, auch das können wir nicht ändern, und nur hoffen, dass er später seinen Weg macht. Er war gerade in seiner Firma stellungs-/gehaltsmäßig vorwärts gekommen. Für Lotti bedeutet es eine starke Veränderung ihres Lebens und leider auch Sorgen, wenigstens bis zu der Zeit, wo sie hoffentlich eine nette Mitbewohnerin für ihre Wohnung gefunden hat, allein kann sie die Wohnung nicht halten. – Dieser Brief, lieber Onkel, wird erst abgesandt werden, wenn wir nicht mehr am Leben sind. Ich hoffe und wünsche, dass uns der Schritt, den wir uns reichlich überlegt haben, gelingen wird, und wir dann diesem schauerlichen Erdendasein entronnen sind.

Wir bitten Dich, dann unsere Kinder – Du hast die Adressen von allen, zu unterrichten – vielleicht telegraphisch, Du hast ja auch die Telegramm-Geschäftsadresse von Lotti.

Ich möchte Dir noch einmal danken für alle Freundlichkeiten und verwandtschaftlichen Gefühle, die Du ein langes Leben lang für mich gehabt hast, die Du mir auch immer wieder zu Teil werden ließest. – Ich bitte Dich: Übertrage sie auch auf unsere Kinder, die schwer genug an dem Schritt zu tragen haben werden, den wir vor haben zu gehen. Vergiss bitte nie, dass sie die Enkel Deiner prachtvollen Schwester Hermine sind, unseres Muttchens.

Noch eine Bitte, lieber Onkel, ich glaube nicht, dass Alex einmal den gleichen Weg gehen wird, den wir vor haben, versuche ihn zu Dir oder ins Ausland drüben zu bekommen, ich würde es Euch beiden wünschen!
Lebe wohl, lieber Onkel, behalte uns in guter Erinnerung, lasse es Dir recht, recht gut gehen, so wie Du es in so reichem Masse verdienst. – Dank noch einmal für alles! Noch einen warmen Händedruck von

Deiner Nichte
/s/ Lucie

Dear Uncle Ferdinand!
I still have to thank you for your recent letter – no, it was a postcard that you wrote shortly after your return from Zurich. – I am glad that you had some relaxation and diversion. – I hope that you will retain your physical and mental health for a long time. – About us I can only tell you that we have reached the end of our strength, what has assaulted us in the last weeks and continues to assault us is again too much. I suppose that you are informed of everything. – We have long endured bravely, but there are in fact things one cannot handle, at least we cannot! – I really don't think that you truly have a precise idea of the position Paul had achieved here and how highly he was esteemed and thought of. If he reads this, he will, with all his modesty, again say, "What nonsense!!" – But how much recognition and esteem Paul received here is proven even today by friends who, despite everything, stand by him faithfully. We led a happy life until '33, and we can be glad that our children got out before the worst time, and could begin to settle down, one hopes that they will continue to make their way, and that their lives will bring them happiness and not all too many cares. That is also my hope today for Hilde, Franz and Inge! – Helmut probably is already in uniform, that, too, we cannot change and can only hope that he will make his way later. He just had advanced in his firm with regard to position and salary. For Lotti this means a considerable change in her life and, unfortunately, worries, at least until such time as, one hopes, she has found a nice girl with whom to share her apartment, by herself she cannot afford it. – This letter, dear Uncle, will only be sent when we are no longer alive. I hope and wish that we will be successful in taking this step, which we have thought about fully, and that we will then have escaped this terrifying earthly existence.

We ask you that you then inform our children of everything – you have their addresses – perhaps by telegram, for you also have Lotti's telegram business address.

I would like to thank you once again for all your friendly deeds and the family feelings that you have had for me all your life and have bestowed on me again and again. – I beg you: transfer them also to our children, who will bear heavy enough a load with the path that we are planning to go on. Please never forget that they are the grandchildren of your splendid sister Hermine, our "little mother."

One more thing I ask for, dear Uncle, I don't think that Alex will some day take the same path that we have decided on, try to bring him to you or abroad overseas, I would wish it for you both!

Farewell, dear Uncle, keep us favorably in your memory, and may you have that truly good life that you so richly deserve. – Thanks again for everything! And finally a warm handshake from

your niece
/s/ Lucie

Letter from Paul Salomon to Professor Rudolf Laun, Hamburg (September 21st, 1941)

Verehrter Herr Professor.
Wir sollten Ihrer freundlichen Absicht nach morgen zu Ihnen kommen; das wird nun leider nicht mehr möglich sein, da wir, überzeugt von der Unmöglichkeit des Weiterlebens unter jetzigen und besonders unter künftigen Verhältnissen heute Abend den hoffentlich gelingenden Versuch machen werden, aus dem Leben zu scheiden. Der beifolgende Brief vom 19/8 zeigt Ihnen, dass unser Entschluss nicht erst heute gefasst ist. Erweisen Sie und Ihre liebe Gattin uns bitte den letzten Liebesdienst, hier im Hause mit nach dem Rechten zu sehen; dazu wird es nützlich sein, wenn Sie sich ungesäumt mit unseren Testamentsvollstreckern, den Herren Rud. Herms, in Firma H. A. Jonas Söhne & Co. und Herrn Dr. Rudolphi sowie mit dem von uns bestimmten Universalerben, Herrn Cornelius von Berenberg Gossler, in Firma Wilh. Ree jr. hier, in Verbindung setzen. Und noch für einen Punkt erbitten wir Ihr freundliches Interesse. Es könnte ja sein, dass das Nachlassgericht unsere Universalerben-Bestimmung aus denkbaren Gründen nicht anerkennt; in diesem Falle haben wir, um zu vermeiden, dass Vermögen etc. dem Staate anheimfällt, den Wunsch, dass der Bruder meiner Frau, Herr Alex. Königswerther, Berlin-Pankow, Florastr. 59, unser Testament anficht, weil er als einziger überlebender nächster Verwandter durch unsere Bestimmungen geschädigt würde. Freilich kennen wir leider seine Absichten bezüglich der Zukunft nicht. Bitte beraten Sie alles mit unseren anderen Freunden.

Und nun noch einen letzten Gruß. Wir danken Ihnen von Herzen für alle Freundschaft und bitten Sie wie Kurt, Ihre Freundschaft unseren Kindern für alle Zukunft zu erhalten.

Ihr
P. Salomon

Es unterschreibt und unterstreicht alles
Ihre für alle Liebe & Freundschaft so dankbare
Lucie Salomon

Esteemed Professor [Laun, Kurt's father]:

In accordance with your kind intention we should be visiting you tomorrow; regrettably that will no longer be possible, as, convinced of the impossibility to continue living under present and especially future conditions, we shall this evening make the attempt – we hope successfully – to depart this life. The enclosed letter of 8/19 shows you that our decision was not just taken today. [That letter is no longer extant.] We ask you and your dear wife to do us the last kindness to take part in looking after things here in the house; to that end it will be useful for you to establish immediate contact with the executors of our will, Messrs. Rud. Herms[20] in the firm of HA. Jonas Sons & Co. and Dr. Rudolphi,[21] as well as with the sole legatee designated by us, Mr. Cornelius von Berenberg-Gossler, of the firm Wilh. Ree jr., of this city. And for one further item we ask your kind intervention. It could happen, after all, that the probate court for conceivable reasons would not consent to our designation of our legatee; in that case we wish – so as to prevent funds etc. from devolving to the state – my wife's brother, Mr. Alex. Koenigswerther, Berlin-Pankow, Florastraße 59, to contest our last will on the grounds that as sole surviving closest relative he would be harmed by our testamentary arrangements. To be sure, we regrettably do not know his intentions with respect to the future. Please consult our other friends for everything. And now at last a final greeting! We thank you with all our heart for all your friendship and ask you and Kurt to continue to extend your friendship to our children for all future times.

Your
P. Salomon

With much gratitude for all love and friendship
all the above is emphatically approved of by your
Lucie Salomon

Letter from Paul Salomon to Dr. Sohege, Hamburg, 21 September, 1941:[22]

Esteemed Doctor.

My wife and I have exhausted our ability to resist the suffering and torment that have befallen us. This evening we shall make the – successful, we hope – attempt to end our lives with Veronal. Be so kind as to confirm our hoped-for death, but for God's sake to make no attempts to recall us into life, should that opportunity seem to present itself. – Our executor will take care of all necessary requirements.

With sincere gratitude,
P. Salomon

On the parents' bedside table Dr. Sohege, summoned at 8:15 the next morning by Marie Seebach, the housekeeper,[23] found a slip of paper containing Vati's final notice:

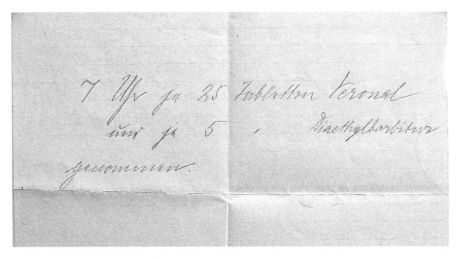

7 o'clock each took 25 pills Veronal and 5 pills Diethylbarbitur.

An entry in the police report states:

This deed may be presumed to be the result of melancholy.

Even though the U.S. was still at peace, preparations for its possible participation in the war had begun. In mid-August of 1941, having previously complied with my obligation to register for the draft, I received a summons from Local Board No. 51 of the Selective Service (which I think I reported to my parents): "You are hereby directed to report to City Hospital Dispensary at 525 E. 80 St. for physical examination at 7 p.m., on Aug. 20, '41." This was the harbinger of my becoming a draftee and, since potential draftees were normally given only a couple of weeks between the final notice and the date of induction, I began to prepare for the second major change in my life.

I suppose it was largely due to these circumstances that I got pretty soused on September 22 at an office party, the occasion for which I no longer remember, somewhere in lower midtown. In part it may also have been loneliness; I was, after all, quite low on the institutional totem pole and didn't have many people to talk to. After I left, I was unsteady and then increasingly nauseous. I finally threw up dramatically against the northern foundation of the Empire State Building – drained and relieved, I made my way home. It was early evening and to my surprise I saw not only Lotti, but also her friend with whom she had shared the apartment; the atmosphere was glum and despondent. When she came home, Lotti had found a telegram under the door, the contents of which had caused her to phone her friend for company and succor. She was crying. The wire, which, alas, doesn't exist any more, informed her of our parents' suicide. It evidently had somehow come from my mother's Uncle Ferdinand, until recently a very wealthy man, who had fled to Zurich after living in Vienna and Prague. Hildi and Franz received the following message through the agency of the Red Cross:

Senden Euch vor Abreise innigste Abschiedsgrüsse und wünschen Euch aus tiefstem Herzen Gesundheit und Glück für alle Zukunft. In steter Liebe Eure endlich befreiten

Vamu.

Before our departure we send you our most loving farewell greetings and our heartfelt wishes for health and good fortune for all future times. With our constant love, your

Vamu, freed at last.

Paul and Lucia Salomon's final message to Hilde and Franz Friedlaender, delivered through the Red Cross

For the facts detailed in this paragraph Lotti and I have no documentation, if indeed there ever was any. Uncle Oskar, the doctor, presumably had supplied the family (in Gera, Halle, and Hamburg – and perhaps Berlin) with Veronal, an overdose of which would be comfortably lethal. It seems that the entire family simultaneously took the same action, except Uncle Alex, who committed suicide in 1942. (Mutti's elder sister, Aunt Elli, had died a natural death sometime earlier.) Tante Fränze, the oldest and clearly the toughest of them all, is said to have pulled through to an unknown span of life in the so-called *Altersghetto* (senior ghetto) of Theresienstadt, where she was reputed (by whom?) to have assumed somewhat of a leadership role – of what and how long is unknown to us, as are the date and place of her death.

Vati had made a hand-written list of political and military events from the 25th of August ("Various threats by Germany. [...]") to the 7th of September, 1939, followed by entries for the fourteenth and thirtieth of the month. ("Campaign in Poland ended; Poland totally destroyed. [...]") Having kept the sheet in his desk, he picked it up again in September 1941 to add the following entries (my translation).

> Cancellation of telephone. 20% levy on capital held by Jews; later raised to 25%. Confiscation of gold, silver, and jewels – minimal reimbursement. Confiscation of radio – without any payment. Take it there in person! Going to theaters, concerts, movies, etc. forbidden. Prohibition of any occupational activity. No further issuance of coupons for clothing. Establishment of separate shops for Jews; partly poor supplies, partly usury. Denial of all special allocations, such as tea, coffee etc. Not even legumes! Purchases of fish, venison and fruit (and fish products) dependent on ration card denied to Jews. – Social-adjustment levy: again 15% of gross income! Medical treatment and hospitals restricted [forbidden?]. Increasing residential aggravations. Automobiles forbidden! Security regulation [?]. Limitation of consumption. Attachment of capital for securing tax on flight from the *Reich*. Class-I taxation. Abolition of all tax exemption. Class-I taxation – as against class III amounts to an increase of c. 75%. Local authorities want to requisition a room [doubtless because of the air-raid September 15–16; see below] Mandatory Jewish identity labels on clothing. Travel forbidden. In Halle [i.e. his sisters] [notice of] obligatory transfer to old age home [for Jews – this meant Theresienstadt].

Paul Samomon's hand-written list of political events at the beginning of the war in 1939 and during the persecution of Jews in September 1941

To try to imagine the state of mind and soul of my parents in anticipation of the final act of their married life is both terrifying and impossible. It gives a particular definition to the expression "death with dignity," and forces one to welcome their decision. I have always hoped that they were blessed with simultaneous dormition. They were buried in the Jewish part of the beautiful cemetery in Ohlsdorf, an outlying district of Hamburg, where Vati had occasionally taken his Sunday walk, when he didn't feel like walking in the nearer city park – also a beautiful wooded area, not far from the *Johanneum*. Uncle Alex wrote us that the burial was attended by

Der Polizeipräsident	Hamburg, den 24.September 1941
V 4. 2743 /4. 12.	Fernsprecher: 34 10 00 und 36 12 31
Polizeiamt	Nebenstelle 21 23
Dienststelle Bergedorf	**Todesanzeige** Sterberegister Nr. 12 /4

Volle Vor- und Familiennamen des Verstorbenen:	Paul Israel Salomon
Beruf des Verstorbenen	fr. Bankdirektor i.R.
Berufsstellung (unter Angabe ob selbständig, Angestellter, Arbeiter, Beamter des öffentlichen Dienstes)	-
Gewerbe oder Betrieb, in dem der Verstorbene tätig war	-
Geburtstag, -monat und -jahr	29.6. 1865
Geburtsort, Kreis	Halle a.Saale
Angabe des Standesamts und der Registernummer	
Staatsangehörigkeit	deutsch
Wohnort	hier, St.Benedictstrasse 29, ptr.
Religion (bei ungetauftem Kind Religion der Eltern)	(ohne Vater Mutter)
Familienstand (ledig, verheiratet, geschieden oder verwitwet)	verheiratet
Wenn verheiratet, Tag der Eheschließung	11.7. 1904 -St.A.Charlottenburg
Volle Vor- u. Familiennamen und Geburtstag und -jahr des überlebenden Ehegatten	Martha Lucia Sarah geb.Königswerther
Ob am Leben oder verstorben	verstorben
Stand oder Gewerbe (unter Angabe ob selbständig, Gehilfe usw.)	-
Wohnort letzter	Hamburg
Wenn Ehefrau überlebender Teil, Angabe ob minderjährig	
Volle Vor- und Familiennamen des Vaters:	David Salomon
Ob am Leben oder verstorben	verstorben
Stand oder Gewerbe	Kaufmann
Wohnort letzter	unbekannt
Volle Vor- und Familiennamen der Mutter:	Mathilde geb. Frank
Ob am Leben oder verstorben	verstorben
Wohnort letzter	unbekannt
Bei unehelicher Geburt auch Gewerbe der Mutter, u. falls verwitwet oder geschieden, Tag des Todes des Mannes oder der Scheidung	
Zahl der hinterlassenen Kinder insgesamt:	3 , davon sind unmündig -
Hierunter aus früheren Ehen	- , davon sind unmündig -
Gesamtzahl der in der letzten Ehe geborenen Kinder (einschließlich Totgeburten)	3
Ort des Todes (oder des Auffindens)	hier St.Benedictstrasse 29,p.
Jahr, Tag, Stunde des Todes (oder des Auffindens)	19 41 , 22.9. , 8,15 Uhr
Todesursache	Schlafmittelvergiftung,Selbstmord

Death record of Paul Salomon, criminal investigation department Hamburg (September 24th, 1941)

Der Polizeipräsident	Hamburg, den 24. 9. 1941
V 4. 2744/41 2.	Fernsprecher: 34 10 00 und 36 12 31
Polizeiamt	Nebenstelle 21 23
Dienststelle Bergedorf	13

Todesanzeige   Sterberegister Nr. /4

Volle Vor- und Familiennamen des Verstorbenen:	Martha Lucia Sarah Salomon geb. Königswerther
Beruf des Verstorbenen	Ehefrau
Berufsstellung (unter Angabe ob selbständig, Angestellter, Arbeiter, Beamter des öffentlichen Dienstes)	-
Gewerbe oder Betrieb, in dem der Verstorbene tätig war	-
Geburtstag, -monat und -jahr	20.12. 1880
Geburtsort, Kreis	Leipzig
Angabe des Standesamts und der Registernummer	
Staatsangehörigkeit	deutsch
Wohnort	hier, St. Benedictstrasse 29, ptr.
Religion (bei ungetauftem Kind Religion der Eltern)	(ohne Vater Mutter)
Familienstand (ledig, verheiratet, geschieden oder verwitwet)	verheiratet
Wenn verheiratet, Tag der Eheschließung	11.7. 1904 -St.A.Charlottenburg, Reg. 367
Volle Vor- u. Familiennamen und Geburtstag und -jahr des überlebenden Ehegatten	Paul Israel Salomon
Ob am Leben oder verstorben	verstorben
Stand oder Gewerbe (unter Angabe ob selbständig, Gehilfe usw.)	Bankdirektor i.R.
Wohnort letzter	Hamburg
Wenn Ehefrau überlebender Teil, Angabe ob minderjährig	
Volle Vor- und Familiennamen des Vaters	Adolf Heinrich Königswerther
Ob am Leben oder verstorben	verstorben
Stand oder Gewerbe	Rentner
Wohnort letzter	unbekannt
Volle Vor- und Familiennamen der Mutter	Hermine geb. Bloch
Ob am Leben oder verstorben	verstorben
Wohnort letzter	unbekannt
Bei unehelicher Geburt auch Gewerbe der Mutter, u. falls verwitwet oder geschieden, Tag des Todes des Mannes oder der Scheidung	
Zahl der hinterlassenen Kinder insgesamt	3 , davon sind unmündig -
Hierunter aus früheren Ehen	- , davon sind unmündig
Gesamtzahl der in der letzten Ehe geborenen Kinder (einschließlich Totgeburten)	3
Ort des Todes (oder des Auffindens)	hier, St. Benedictstrasse 29
Jahr, Tag, Stunde des Todes (Auffindens)	19 41 22. 9. 8:15 Uhr
Todesursache	Schlafmittelvergiftung, Selbstmord

Abt. V.
Vordruck 5. E/0405   Wenden!

Death record of Lucia Salomon, criminal investigation department Hamburg (September 24th, 1941) a fair number of mourners, Jewish and non-Jewish – the former seamstress, their elderly domestic employee (Jews could not employ non-Jewish female domestics under the age of 45 because of the "potential danger of *Rassenschande*" [racial pollution]), von Berenberg-Goßler, Kurt Laun's parents and others. Uncle Alex took a hand in the dissolution of the household; their possessions were sold.

They were an exemplary couple, whose goodness, patriotism, and virtue were ill rewarded.

HISTORICAL BACKGROUND

A couple of years ago I received from Walter Eberstadt (long a New York resident) a small German paperback, entitled *Die Deportation der Hamburger Juden 1941-1945*.[24] The most remarkable of its four grueling essays seems to me to be the first, by Frank Bajohr: "'... *dann bitte keine Gefühlsduseleien.' Die Hamburger and die Deportationen.*"[25] The quotation ('... please no exaggerated sentimentality') in the title comes from the printed news bulletin of the Hamburg NSDAP (Nazi party office) for October 1941.[26] The exhortation against emotional weakness concerns any citizen's treacherous compassion towards the incipient deportation of Jews.

Before quoting two translated passages from Bajohr's essay (pp. 19–21, 25–26 – notes omitted) I list relevant events in the late summer and fall of 1941.

September 1:	Publication of the decree regarding the compulsory wearing of the *Judenstern* (yellow star with *"Jude"* across its center).
September 15–16:	English aerial bombardment renders more than 600 citizens of Hamburg homeless.
Mid-September:	Hitler's decision to have Germany "as soon as possible emptied and liberated of Jews from West to East."[27]
September 19:	Effective date for the obligatory wearing by Jews of the *Judenstern*. It seems, therefore, that my parents, surely not willing to expose

	themselves to this indignity, stayed home for the last three days of their lives.)
October 14:	Official order to begin the deportation of all Jews from Germany.
October 17:	Gestapo orders the deportation of 1000 Hamburg Jews to Lodz ("Litzmannstadt"); 1075 Jews were actually chosen.
October 22:	Designated Jews receive deportation orders in the mail. – 41 suicides.
October 24:	Deportees to report for deportation the next day.
October 24–25:	"[...] during the night [...] pent up in the cellars of the lodge building."[28]
October 25:	1034 Jews deported.
December 6:	2128 additional (altogether more than half of Hamburg's) Jews deported
By the end of the war:	7812 Jewish victims in Hamburg, 308 of them classed as suicides.

I. The principal actor in the correspondence excerpted below is the "Higher SS and Police Leader" Rudolf Querner, writing on 31 October, 1941, to Karl Kaufmann, the *Gauleiter* – provincial leader – of Hamburg, who is temporarily in Garmisch-Partenkirchen, a popular mountain resort in southern Bavaria.

In this letter Querner informs […] his "dear Karl" in terse words, that "the next transport of Jews, which was supposed to go off tomorrow, has been postponed for a week because of equipment shortages. Advantageous, giving us a bit more time for preparations."

Like all passages concerning deportation and holocaust in Querner's correspondence, this excerpt is embedded among much lengthier news items, which sound like the sort of banal messages one would write on a vacation postcard. Greetings "from Raimund," Kaufmann's adjutant, [...] an invitation to a "comradely meeting" of the Hamburg hunters' group [...], a short report on the recent jovial meeting of the police, news about his intention to invite a straw-widower colleague [...] for dinner, finally best wishes for a good vacation [...] and "my compliments to your wife. Best regards and Heil Hitler – Yours, Rudolf."

Woven, with few words, into this chain of banalities is the monstrosity – the deportation, which recedes into the background of an evocation of a putative "normality." [...] In the context of cozy conviviality, the rupture of civilization shriveled into a marginal news item.

This, however, should not lead to the mistaken conclusion that the collaborators were unaware of the consequences of their actions. For instance, as early as October 1941 Querner was involved in plans for the construction in Mogilev (Russia) of a death camp complete with gas chamber and had inspected (suitable) local areas together with Himmler. His correspondence shows Querner to be informed about all essential aspects of the impending murders. This is elucidated by correspondence with the Hamburg police sergeant Fritz Jacob, who took part in the murder of the Jewish population of Kamenets-Podolskiy (Ukraine). The shootings, combined with his separation from his family, caused psychological difficulties for Jacob, which he hinted at in a letter to Querner of May 1942: "Sometimes one could feel like bawling. It isn't good to love children as much as I did."

This caused Querner to send the Hamburg police sergeant a "comradely admonition" to show greater toughness. Jacob instantly responded with a second letter. Concerned about being thought a weakling he wrote:

"I thank you for your message of exhortation. You are indeed right. We men of the new Germany must be hard on ourselves, even in the face of a longer separation from the family. After all, the issue is now to settle accounts, once and for all, with the war criminals, so as to establish a more beautiful and eternal Germany for our offspring. We're not sleeping here. Three to four operations a week. One time gypsies and another time Jews, partisans, and similar riffraff. It's great that we now have a branch of the SD [*Sicherheitsdienst*, i.e. Security Police]; our collaboration is first-rate [...]. Whenever a misdeed requires instant expiation, one contacts the SD, and righteous justice commences instantly. By way of ordinary jurisdiction it wouldn't be possible to exterminate an entire family, when only the father is the culprit [...]. Well, of the Jewlets [*Jüdlein*] living just here in Kamenets-Podolskiy there now remains only a minute percentage of the original 24,000 [...]. We stay the course without remorse, and then '... for the peace of the world's sake it is that the waves break.'"

Querner, writing once again, complied with Jacob's concluding request for occasional "heart-warming news from home" in a letter of August 1942, assuring him that "above all I'm delighted that you understood my comradely admonition just as I meant it."

When some years ago I read this correspondence in the Federal Archives, this blatant exhibition of unscrupulousness and brutality took my breath away. These men weren't desk-bound functionaries, but murderers, who knew exactly what they were doing and acknowledged it frankly and fully. Not only did Querner show that he was precisely informed about the murders, he also, adducing an ideological goal, required his subordinates to carry them out with unscrupulous severity. The participants were quite aware – as is indicated by Jacob's remark about the absence of "ordinary jurisdiction" – that their actions put them beyond the pale of widely prevailing legal and ethical norms.

II. Yet, this look at the comportment of Hamburg's populace would not be complete without mention of that minute minority which, despite public threats, involved itself on behalf of individual deportees. Ingrid Weckerhas reported that private individuals or firms anonymously donated quite large supplies of food for the deportees, such as bread, butter, sausages, sugar, crates of wine, and candy for the children.[29] The Hamburg banker Cornelius von Berenberg-Goßler [my parents' legatee] was one of those who went to considerable trouble to assist Jewish citizens. The diary of mayor Carl Vincent Krogmann contains specific entries of names of people asking him [in vain, because his hands were tied] to intercede on behalf of particular individuals.

The Protestant pastor Seyfarth even wrote straight to Himmler, to forestall the deportation of a 93-year-old lady. Here is a contemporary report on the futility of his efforts and its consequences for Seyfarth:

"Six months after sending his petition he received a reply in the form of a summons to the Gestapo in Hamburg. There, in an easy-chair sat a young SS-man, who didn't even offer a seat to the old man, wearing his many medals and honorific decorations. He got a terrible dressing-down and was told that it was inconceivable for him as a German to stick up for Jews. When he pointed out that the old "lady" of nearly 93 years after all hadn't really done anything to anybody, he was given to understand that this was no lady, but a "Jew woman!" [...] [He was admonished] never again to be in touch with Jews who might still be around; otherwise he would without fail be sent off immediately to a concentration camp."

Some months after completion of this essay Marion chose to re-examine the historical materials that had accumulated during our fifty years of marriage. Among them were the many lengthy letters I had written my sister Lotti and her husband during my post-war service in Germany, both as a soldier and subsequently as a civilian. To complement Bajohr's essay I quote the following passage from a letter I wrote in November 1945.

In Russia Otto [Kurt Laun's brother] had to spend a night with an SD [*Sicherheitsdienst*] outfit, called *Sonderkommando 7a*. In the course of the conversation during dinner he found out that the unit was charged with the *"regelmäßig anfallenden Erschießungen"* [regularly occurring shootings]. He said to the man next to him (who seemed perfectly normal and O.K. to him) that he supposed those shootings involved deserters and similar cases. He was enlightened that they "took care" of Jews, persons who were suspected enemies of the Reich, and partisans. After overcoming his initial shock Otto said, "All right, you shoot a partisan; what happens to his wife and children?" Oh, they shoot the wife, too; if the husband was a partisan, his wife could be assumed to be one, too. And what happened to the innocent children, Otto wanted to know. He was informed by his host in an entirely amiable manner that he didn't have to worry, *"da verschwende ich keine Munition, die mach' ich mit dem Pistolenknauf tot"* ["in those cases I waste no ammunition; them I kill off with my pistol grip."] [...] Otto made a report to his Corps G-2, who forwarded it to the Army, where they claimed never to have heard of the unit before. Army Group knew about it, but admitted that they were unable to do anything about it, since the unit operated under direct orders from Berlin (Himmler).

REFLECTIONS

The classic story of an individual's ideological and racial perversion is Joseph Conrad's wondrously wordy, crepuscular *Heart of Darkness* ("Exterminate all the brutes!¹" – "... those heads on the stakes ..." – "... he was hollow at the core." – "The Horror! The Horror!" – "The offing was barred ..."), a visionary fictionalized tale of perverted colonial arrogance and the dusk of civilization, published in 1902 at the very beginning of the 20th century. It is hard to imagine a grosser, more pervasive corruption of nationalistic ideology on a national scale than the Nazis' persecution and destruction of Jews, its unspeakable cruelty resulting from the mixture of debased idealism and hateful prejudice. All too many people in Germany – apart from fanatics and plain scoundrels – did not (or in their consternation chose not to) see the evil until it was too late. The virulent extent of such moral and civic ruination exceeds the foresight of reflective people, and so the momentum reaches the point of no return. Even my good father at first hesitantly felt compelled to concede that a result of Hitler's radical political and economic moves was the proven lifting of the pervasive economic and psychic depression in Germany. More than once I had heard him express the uncomprehendingly ethical fantasy – and he was not the only one – that if somehow perhaps good people, Germans first and secondly Jewish, could manage to present themselves to Hitler, he might well be persuaded of the erroneousness of the anti-semitic part of his political dogma. To many people the depth of the Nazis' ideological depravity was simply and honorably inconceivable. Some "Aryans," von Berenberg-Gossler among them, joined the Nazi party early in 1933, hoping that they might be effective in exerting a moderating influence;

but when that inevitably turned out to be a wishful fantasy, few had his upright courage to resign from the party, as he did in the summer of 1934. After the beginning of the war the fear that dissent would be treated as political as well as ideological treason necessarily became overwhelming, and most initial moderates got swept along into the maelstrom of the dominant excess; my mother even advised Kurt Laun's father to join the Nazi party so as to avoid difficulties. Inevitably a possessed leader at the opportune historical moment possesses his followers. To put it with restraint – and with due respect to Pastor Hunzinger – the prospects for the change from the (tainted) glories of Western civilization to enlightened global compatibility without religious, ideological, or commercial excesses, are not improving at the beginning of the 21st century.

The correspondence of Querner and Jacob reminded me that sometime in 1934 our *Klassenlehrer* in an excess of somewhat risky thinking mentioned that we might find it interesting to read a book, published in 1932 in a series to which he himself had in 1933 contributed his translation of Plutarch's *Lives*. The book was a German translation of Gustave LeBon's (1841–1931) *La Psychologie des Foules* (The Psychology of the Masses), published seven years before Conrad's novel. LeBon has the reputation of having been a "racist," like so many others of the time. (I remember the husband of one of Lotti's friends, a Jewish Viennese psychiatrist trained by Freud, being, in his superior innocence, nonplussed and a bit amused, on his arrival in New York in 1939, by the existence and appearance of "Negroes" in Western clothes.) But many of his insights – I quote a mere handful – are startlingly on the mark.[30]

> All rulers of the earth, all founders of religions and realms, the apostles of all creeds, the most outstanding statesmen, and, in more modest spheres, the leaders of small societies have always been unconscious psychologists with instinctive and often very sure knowledge of the mass psyche; because they knew it so well, it was easy for them to seize power. (6)
>
> In the communal psyche individual rational capabilities and, hence, personalities are effaced. Heterogeneity is absorbed into homogeneity, and the subconscious predominates. (15)
>
> To engender belief – be it religious, political, or social – i.e. belief in a person or an idea is the great leader's particular role. (99)
>
> Crimes committed by masses are, as a rule, the consequence of strong suggestion, and individual participants are later convinced, [properly] to have obeyed a duty. (138)

It is terrifying to consider how much power a man achieves who knows how to acquire a nimbus, as he blends strong conviction with unusual rational limitation. But those are the necessary preconditions for overcoming impediments and to achieve potency of will [*um wollen zu können*]. Instinctively masses recognize in persons of such powerful conviction the masters they need. (171)

"Das hört nicht auf, nie hört das auf." (That doesn't end, never will it end.)[31]

One month after my parents' murder by proxy I began my military service. I visited their grave in 1966.

EPILOGUE

In 1979 the *Johanneum* celebrated its 450th anniversary, which Marion and I attended with much pleasure. Those of my classmates who had survived the war came with their wives to take part in the festivities, including Victor Hadamczik, the erstwhile leader of the class, who was moved nearly to tears by Marion's and my participation in the event.

Twenty-five years later the *Johanneum* chose – surprisingly – to mark its 475th anniversary with at least equal pomp and circumstance, as it happened, about a month after I had finished the preceding essay. Five of us were left to attend, but only two (including myself) stayed through the three days of the main celebrations. Monday morning (24 May, the school's birthday) there was a festive Protestant service in the magnificent Baroque *Michaeliskirche,* where as an adolescent I had heard performances of Bach's *Passions.* This time the school's chorus and orchestra provided music, and the pastor's sermon as well as remarks by others not only evoked the city's distant and more recent past, but also emphasized the school's continuing adherence to its pedagogical mission.

In the afternoon there was a select reception in Hamburg's magnificently ornate late-nineteenth-century *Rathaus* (City Hall), with many enlightening speeches. Two days later the school offered an evening concert, with the student instrumentalists and choristers, in contrast to earlier times, nearly equally composed of boys and girls, looking fresh-faced and mostly having characteristically Northern complexions and hair-color. It was an event – in the school hall (the *Aula),* where I had graduated two thirds of a century earlier – that I wouldn't have wanted to miss, even though the qualities of the performances certainly varied. The stunning high point was the performance by three siblings and one unrelated student of the first movement of Beethoven's String Quartet, op. 18, no. 4, led by the youngest of the family – not yet 10; the entirely professional playing was phenomenal.

Intense nostalgia marked the intervening two days. Even the not exactly welcoming weather – no rain, but invigoratingly chilly, cloudy, and windy – forcefully evoked the distant past. I experienced Hamburg this time with unforeseen intensity. No prejudice colors my assertion that it is surely one of the world's most beautiful and livable cities. The vistas created by the many expanses of water – the *Außenalster* primarily, but also the *Binnenalster,* the numerous more or less hidden canals, the *Elbe* area with its old, far from rectilinear streets and the fair number of surviving centuries-old narrow houses (some built right into the very edge of canals), as well as the spaciousness of some of the "downtown" quarters with their tastefully elegant window displays, and the palatial bank building in which my father had worked – many of those sites and areas still display the hard-earned and well-mannered opulence that was even more in evidence during my youth. And most striking – the blessings of the season: the second half of May brings forth the flowering of Hamburg's abundant greenery, especially in the residential areas: the ubiquitous chestnut trees are loaded with the innumerable candelabras of their blossoms – most white, some pink – and rhododendrons and lilacs bloom everywhere, offset by the golden flowering pendants of the *Goldregen* (golden rain or laburnum) trees.

I had noticed this floral profusion right after my arrival, but was quite overwhelmed by it when, after visiting my parents' grave, I took a long, partly sunny walk through Hamburg's famous spacious cemetery (reputedly the world's largest), in effect a meticulously maintained wooded and flowered park. As I walked about that day and in the city park and elsewhere the next, on the clean earthen or gravel paths, just as my father had done on most Sundays, the intensity of nostalgic feeling and the recognition of the inevitable loss (and compensating gain) more than 65 years past hit me – a foreigner quartered in a hotel – with great poignancy. "My God, what we have lost," I kept thinking, in terms both of human relations of all kinds and of the comforts, amenities, and challenges of a city that – notwithstanding the absence of historical monuments of the more distant past – is beautiful enough a European model of urban civilization to account for naming three of its streets along the *Außenalster: Fernsicht* (Distant View), *Bellevue,* and *Schöne Aussicht* (Beautiful View).

Just a year and a half later I again found myself in Hamburg, having been invited to read from the recently published German edition of this book to a good-sized audience at my old school. That evening's event was preceded in the later morning by a brief ceremony in front of the house in the St. Benediktstraße to dignify the recent installation in the sidewalk of two small brass squares *(Stolpersteine)*, memorializing my parents as former residents and victims of Nazi persecution. Through the great kindness of my publisher, who had planned both occasions, the morning's event was followed by a lunch in the house, in the former *Damenzimmer* (salon). It was an experience both gratifying and bewildering. The ground floor, for instance, had become an office, run by a very kind and personable gentleman, who had made it available for the occasion. The dissonance between the memory of the ambiguously fraught past of the house and the experience of its heterogeneous present is irreconcilable.

NOTES

1 Paul Salomon, b. 29 June 1865, in Halle (Saale), d. 21 September 1941 in Hamburg. *Direktor* (manager – one of three) of the Dresdner Bank in Hamburg. "After graduating from the Gymnasium learned banking at the Halle bank of Kullisch, Kaempf & Co [...] , then served in the Infantry Regiment No. 36 in Halle, then became an employee of the Dresdner Bank in Hamburg and advanced to the position of *Direktor* of that bank. S. is president of the board of the Automatic Telephone Corporation; he is member of the boards of the Hanseatic Credit Corporation for Public Transport, of the Neptunus Assecuranz Company, Hamburg, of the German-West-African Trade Corporation, Hamburg – Hamburg, St. Benedictstraße 27." (*Reichshandbuch der deutschen Gesellschaft* II, 1931).

2 Martha Lucia ("Lucie") Salomon, nee Königswerther, b. 20 December 1880 in Leipzig, d. 21 September 1941 in Hamburg. Parents: Adolf Heinrich Königswerther and Hermine Königswerther, nee Bloch.

3 Hilde Freeman (before emigration: Friedlaender), nee Salomon, 13 April 1906 – 6 January 1999.

4 Lotte Hellman, nee Salomon, b. 22 March 1913; living in Boca Raton, Fl.

5 Marion Sanders, nee Hollaender, b. 14 February 1926 in Berlin; retired journalist (editorial research, Time Magazine); d. 14 May 2007.

6 Nina Sanders, b. 16 May 1959, psychotherapist, New York.

7 Peter Sanders, b. 31 January 1962, cellist, New York City Ballet Orchestra.

8 Alex Königswerther, b. 25 June 1877 in Leipzig, d. 24 August 1942 (suicide), in Berlin.

9 Mathilde Salomon, nee Frank; married to David Salomon, merchant in Halle.

10 The Introduction of Amos Elon's *The Pity of It All* (New York, 2002) gives an informative historical summary of Jewish assimilation in Germany. Its seventh and eighth chapters contain detailed presentations of its historical facets during the first half of my father's life.

11 Harold Hellman, b. 30 May 1908, d. 27 April 2000; Vice-President, Corn Products Corp.

12 Franz Hermann Friedlaender (after emigration: Francis George Freeman).

13 *Das Johanneum,* Mitteilungen des Vereins ehemaliger Schüler der Gelehrtenschule des Johanneums, Hamburg 1981, 79–85.

14 In view of the recently published book by Roger Cohen (*Soldiers and Slaves,* Knopf, New York, 2005), that was an entirely justified decision.

15 *Das Johanneum,* 1982, 79.

16   The house St. Benediktstraße 27 was sold on 31 December 1938, to Herbert A. Böttcher.

17   The translation was made by my sister Lotti for her husband; the original is lost.

18   HFs: Hilde and Franz Friedlaender. – Truderichs: My cousin Erich and his wife Trude.

19   Ferdinand Bloch-Bauer, brother of Hermine Königswerther, my maternal grandmother. Maria Altmann, daughter of her brother Gustav and hence one of my mother's cousins, has repeatedly been in the news recently, having successfully pursued major claims for restitution against Austrian and Swiss institutions.

20   Member of law firm Jonas & Söhne.

21   Walter Julius Rudolphi, City Supreme Court Judge, retired, deported to the Theresienstadt concentration camp on 15 October 1942, probably killed there in 1944.

22   State Archive Hamburg, Polizeiakte, Polizeibehörde – Unnatural Deaths, 1941/1599.

23   Marie Seebach, interviewed by the police, testified that she had been very satisfied with her job, that the parents had a few days earlier talked to her about their intent to commit suicide, and that she had tried to talk them out of it.

24   Forschungsstelle für Zeitgeschichte in Hamburg und Institut für die Geschichte der deutschen Juden, Hamburg, 2000.

25   Frank Bajohr, "'[...] dann bitte keine Gefühlsduseleien.' Die Hamburger und die Deportationen", 13–29; also Ina Lorenz, "Aussichtsloses Bemühen. Die Arbeit der jüdischen Gemeinde 1941–1945," 30–44.

26   Bajohr, p. 22.

27   Bajohr, p. 14.

28   Lorenz, p. 31.

29   Bajohr, n. 39.

30   *Pyschologie der Massen,* Leipzig, 1932.

31   Günther Grass, end of *Im Krebsgang* [Crabwalk], 2002.

CONTENTS

Preface 7

Childhood 9

Youth 25

Emigration 41

The Parents' Life and Death 57

Historical Background 83

Reflections 89

Epilogue 93

Notes 96